All the

NOISE

is in the

SHALLOW END

of the

POOL

For Dianne,

My Sweetheart
My Love
My Swim Buddy

contents

preface

This is the first preface I have ever written. I am, you might say, a literary novice, so green in fact, I honestly didn't know the difference between a preface and an introduction. I had to look it up. A preface, in case you're wondering, is a brief statement written by the author where you "introduce yourself to your readers and explain to them why they should hear what you have to say."[1] Reading that aloud, I wasn't sure where to begin. It's hard enough to be brief. As a pastor, I find it difficult to say "hello" in less than three sentences and that's without the obligatory word study and bit of poetry. Now you're telling me I have to convince my readers to hear what I have to say before I say it? As a happily former salesperson, the very idea makes me uncomfortable. But, as I thought about it, this book needs to start somewhere so, in the spirit of those who have written prefaces time immemorial, I might as well give it a try. Hello. My name is Mark Warner. I'm an author, speaker, storyteller, pastor…tinker, tailor, soldier, spy! Okay, that last part isn't true, but it's way more exciting than anything I could tell you about myself. Besides, this book isn't about you getting to know me better.

You'll learn plenty about my life in the pages that follow and as you do, I think you'll find, I'm just like you, a fellow traveler. Getting to know me won't change your life. It's not about you and me. It's about you and Jesus.

I wrote this book to help you draw closer to Jesus. It's about following His lead, responding to His invitations, attending to His presence, and letting Him love you. It's about moving from familiarity to intimacy, about living out of your true identity, and learning to live freely and lightly as Jesus said you could. If that appeals to you, if you feel even the smallest spark of interest or desire rising within you, if you long for more, then this book is for you. It's a testimony, my testimony, to the "absolutely unconditional, unlimited and unimaginably extravagant love of God."[2] It was, for me, a labor of love, written around the edges of my "day job" over a three-year period. As I wrote, I was thinking of all the people I'd ever had the privilege to pastor, all the people I currently pastor. I was thinking of you. But more importantly, God was thinking of you. He had you in mind when He prompted me to share my story. I wrote hoping my struggle, my search for a deeper, more satisfying life with God, would evoke in you a similar desire. Putting it simply, I aim to tease you forward, out of the shallows of a largely autonomous life into a deeper life lived in growing dependence upon God.

That said, you should know, this is not a book about the deep end of the pool. I may write about that someday, after I've spent more time there, but today is not that day. No, this is a book about how I left the shallows. What precipitated my transition? In short, I reached a crisis in my early fifties. I will talk about that in Chapter 1. It wasn't the first time I grew disillusioned, certainly not the first time I'd been depressed in ministry, but it was memorable because, for the first time in thirty years, I honestly had nothing to be depressed about. My children were happily married. The staff at church was as healthy as it had ever been. And the church itself was booming — new people were finding us, giving was up — there was momentum and we were enjoying the presence of God. Everything was fine, better than fine, fabulous even by almost any measure. Anyone looking in from the outside would have thought I had it all, that I was content, successful, that I had a great relationship with Jesus. I saw myself as a servant of the King, His ambassador. I'd carved out a niche for myself in the shallow end of the pool and I was comfortable, content, fulfilled until…I wasn't.

I wonder if you know what I mean. I wonder if you've ever felt what I felt — that gnawing ache inside you. I wondered, to echo Jim Collins, if the good relationship I had with Jesus was robbing me of something more, the great relationship that might await me in the deep end of the pool. As we begin our time together, you should know, Jesus won't force Himself on anyone. Your ability to draw near to Jesus, attend to Jesus and follow Jesus as one of His intimates depends upon your willingness to listen and respond to His voice. Nineteen times, in Matthew 13 alone, Jesus used the word "hear" or "listen." He said, "Whoever has ears, let them hear (Matthew 13:9)." He said, "Blessed are your eyes because they see, and your ears because they hear (Matthew 13:16)." He's talking about the way God's Kingdom comes among us. It's about our willingness to hear, that the truth is more or less obvious depending upon your willingness to listen. So, let me ask you a personal question, how receptive are you? How open are you to the idea that your current experience of God might not be all there is? How curious are you about what more God might have for you? Curiosity is a very important part of spiritual growth.

It's especially important if, like me, you grew up in a church that emphasized knowing about God over the direct experience of God. Not long ago, I felt prompted to write a post on social media about my experience with the traditional evangelical path of discipleship. In that post I said that this traditional path, with its emphasis on Bible knowledge, sound doctrine and apologetics, is a path that often leads to familiarity with God but not intimacy. That certainly describes my life experience and I've observed something similar in others as well. Here's the thing. I contend that any really healthy relationship requires both — head and heart, knowledge and experience, familiarity and intimacy. That's why I wrote this book. I want to help you bring the two together, to get beyond mere familiarity with God and find true intimacy.

Looking back on my life, I find it remarkable how easily I accepted ideas about God as substitutes for the direct experience of God. It's especially puzzling because I had what I thought was a wealth of experience. I had an angelic encounter at age fifteen, another at age twenty-three. I had experienced the presence of God, heard the voice of God on a handful of occasions. But I was filtering these isolated events through my theological disposition. See, I had an idea about God that God only did stuff like that if He had some pronouncement to make, some major course correction or specific thing He wanted done. Having received His pronouncement, like Mary with the angel Gabriel, I came to never expect anything like that again unless, of course, God had further pronouncements. I was receptive to God's interventions in my life, but I had no room for the ever-presence of God, for the love of God expressed in real time, for daily conversation with God, let alone companionship. I retreated into my ideas about God, content with familiarity. I had made His acquaintance and that, I thought, was as far as it goes. Imagine my surprise when I discovered there's more. Do you want to know the more there is?

I've arranged this book in three sections. The first chapter sets the stage for what's to come. I share a bit of my story, talk about my early years in ministry and the crisis that precipitated the biggest transformation of my life. The second and third chapters, *Training, Not Just Trying* and *Drawn, No Longer Driven*, explain the fundamental change that radically altered my approach to a life with God and sent me on a journey of discovery. Chapters four through seven, then, are the truths that came home to me as I responded to God. They form the foundation for the free and light life Jesus said I could have, the life He offers us all.

As you turn the page, I want to encourage you to keep reading. God has something for you in the pages of this book. I wouldn't presume to know what exactly, but I know He put it in your hands for a reason. He is with you. What's more, He likes you, He loves you, and He loves loving you.

Mark Victor Warner
January, 2025

one

A Life of Sundays

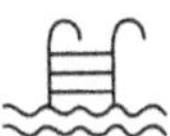

It was a sultry afternoon in late summer. The sun-drenched pavement beneath my bare feet radiated with a message that wouldn't be ignored — *run*! We were going to the pool, the barely bigger-than-a-postage-stamp pool that was a prominent feature of every roadside motel in those days. My family was on vacation, a rarity for us, and after a long day riding the hump in the middle of the backseat, fending off the razor-sharp elbows of my seat-hogging brothers, I was ready to blow off some steam.

The memory of that afternoon has faded a bit, but some things never leave you entirely. Brimming with excitement, I broke formation and ran ahead. I can still hear my mom calling, imploring me to stop, but the simmering pot of my anticipation had finally boiled over. I had had enough for one day — enough travel without air conditioning, enough middle kid in the middle seat, enough Stuckey's pecan candy to last me a lifetime. I had one thing on my mind and one thing only. I was going swimming and nothing could stop me.

Throwing open the gate, I dropped my armload of swim paraphernalia and, without thinking, leapt for the water. Surely, I don't need to tell you how it feels when you suddenly realize you're in over your head. We've all had similar experiences, all felt the helplessness and fear that envelopes you when you know something terrible is happening and there's nothing you can do about it. That's how I felt that day as I watched the surface of the water disappear above me. I had never been in the deep end of the pool. Truth be told, I don't remember ever being in a pool. I was barely six-years-old and my experience with water was limited to playing in the shallows of Elk Creek, which I loved, and our bathtub on a Saturday night, which I tried to avoid at all costs. The deep end was an unfamiliar experience for me, and I was terrified. My parents had talked about enrolling me in swimming lessons alongside my brother, Dave, but that would come later. At this particular moment, in a nondescript pool surrounded by a chain-link fence in front of a tired motel somewhere between Erie, Pennsylvania and Columbus, Georgia, I was in deep trouble.

This is where the flickering frames of the memory flip back and forth between slow and fast motion. One moment, I'm falling away from safety, confused, gripped by fear, and the next I'm bobbing up out of the water, shouting, sputtering and gasping for air. One moment, I'm thrashing in a ripe panic, far below the surface, only vaguely aware of the muffled shouts above me and the next my hand breaks the surface, straining for purchase on the edge of the pool just barely out of my reach. One moment, darkness is closing in and my all-to-brief life is flashing before my eyes and the next, I awaken to find myself lying in the sunshine looking up at a kindly, older woman who had, I later learned, jumped off her poolside lounge in time to grab my outstretched hand and pull me from the water. As I lay there on my side, coughing up a lung, she gently patted my back and said, "There, there now. You're okay. Everything is okay."

But I wasn't okay. Not really. I was happy to be alive, sure. Even at that age, I was vaguely aware that I had nearly died. I was traumatized, no doubt. But I was also suddenly sensitive to the fact that I didn't have what you might call "deep water skills." I had lots of experience in the shallows. The shallows were my natural habitat. I knew how to faux-swim across the surface while walking along the bottom. I knew how to stand up and get my head above water when I'd inadvertently swallowed a mouthful. I knew how to hold my breath. I'd even mastered the art of opening my eyes underwater, though I never enjoyed it. I had a bag full of shallow water skills. I was a master, you might say, of the shallows, but for all my inch-deep expertise, none of what I knew was adequate to sustain me for long in the deep end of the pool.

My Confession

W.H. Vanstone wrote, "The church is like a swimming pool in which all the noise comes from the shallow end."[3]

Sitting alone in my office, one day in 2012, tears streaming down my face, I was done. The noise — the insistent, unrelenting hubbub in the shallow end of the pool — was crushing me. In that moment, I experienced a kind of spiritual tinnitus as the roar of a thousand disparate voices filled my mind — shouting instructions, making demands, clawing their way forward, vying for my attention. It was overwhelming! I put my head in my hands in a vain attempt to make it stop, but it wouldn't be quieted. Along with the all too familiar voice of the enemy — speaking condemnation, castigating me for my weakness, branding me a failure — were the voices of countless staffers, board members, pastors and parishioners telling me I'd never amount to much. I wasn't meeting their expectations. I wasn't good enough, smart enough, or talented enough. I wasn't a good leader. I didn't care about others. Add that chorus of imprecations to my own voice telling me I should be more successful, I ought to be more compassionate, I should have more friends, I ought to be famous and my deeply embedded desire for the recognition, appreciation and good opinion of others and you might understand my despair. It's a funny thing about the shallow end of the pool. The angry voices, the voices of condemnation, accusation, and self-doubt, always seem to be louder than the voices of encouragement and affirmation. To make matters worse, I have always been one of those people who hates failure far more than he enjoys success.

If the church is like a swimming pool in which all the noise comes from the shallow end, then I'd certainly lived my whole life in the shallows, adding my voice to the cacophonous din. That is my confession. I have lived a very noisy life. I spent years jostling for my place in the shallow end of the pool, rarely content, rarely at peace, always striving, reaching, grasping and I can tell you where it leads. I can tell you how it ends. It ends in disappointment. It ends with the realization, to borrow an image from Stephen Covey, that the ladder you've been climbing all these years is leaning against the wrong wall. It ended, for me, with the crushing weight of expectations and the many voices of condemnation drowning out the voice of God. I could barely hear Him. As a result, I wasn't just thinking about leaving the ministry that day in 2012; I was formulating a plan, excited at the prospect, dreaming about doing something else, anything else. This, for me, was no small step and I'll tell you why.

Stop the Car

It all started in 1976. I was fifteen-years-old and, after a night of riding go-carts and playing putt-putt golf with the church youth group, I was, reluctantly, on my way home in the passenger seat of my friend Tom's 1967 Camaro. It was nigh unto midnight and I was pushing curfew. I knew my parents would be up, anxiously awaiting my return.

As we rolled past the monument on Main Street, Tom and I in front and three other friends wedged in the back, I noticed a commotion on the sidewalk in front of the Western Auto. A young man was standing over a much older man, offering him his hand, trying to help him up. The man on the ground was clearly incapable of helping himself. He kept rolling from side-to-side, trying in vain to grab hold of the Good Samaritan, only to flop back down onto the sidewalk. We were mesmerized. Growing up in the smallest of small towns, we had never seen anything like it before. Tom instinctively slowed the car as we went by, the light of a nearby streetlight suddenly illuminating the face of the fallen man. That's when I realized, to my horror and embarrassment, that the helpless man lying on the sidewalk that night was my grandfather.

He lived in a small, one-room apartment above the hardware store. My mom, the oldest in her family, had insisted he move there so she could look after him. He lost his wife, my grandmother, nine years earlier. She died on my birthday, a victim of breast cancer in her fifties. I barely remember her, but I remember him. He was a jovial man with a quick sense of humor when he was sober and a sad, lonely muddle when he was not. I knew he was an alcoholic. He had struggled with alcohol addiction most of his life. He'd shown up at our home drunk more times than I could count as a child, knowing my parents would take him in, clean him up and get him back on his feet.

That night, my grandfather had gone so far down the rabbit hole he didn't even know who I was. "Stop the car," I said to Tom. "Why?" he asked, turning slowly to look at me. "It's my grandfather," I whispered. A hush came over the car. I was deeply humiliated, but he was still my grandfather, and I loved him. As tempted as I might have been to say nothing, I couldn't just leave him there. "Your grandfather?" Tom asked quizzically. "Yes," I replied impatiently, "It's my grandfather. Stop the car!" Jolted into action, he quickly pulled over and threw it in park. It *was* my grandfather, and he was a hot mess from head to toe.

It's funny the things that stick with you. I can still remember the pungent stench that hung in the air as the three of us — Tom, the stranger and I — got him to his feet and pushed him up the stairs to his apartment. Fishing around in his filthy pants pocket for the key, I opened the door, and we half-walked, half-carried him to the bed. With tears in my eyes, I turned abruptly to leave, herding the others out the door in front of me. "Try to sleep it off," I said roughly over my shoulder. At that moment, my grandfather sat bolt upright in bed and, lucid as you please, called my name. "Mark," he cried out forcefully. Surprised, I spun around to face him. That's when he looked at me sheepishly and said, "You know I'm not a drinking man." I dropped my head to my chest and heaved a sigh. It may seem like an odd thing for him to say in those circumstances, but I knew immediately what he was trying to do. Through the haze of a drunken stupor, he was trying to manage my sinking opinion of him, grasping at straws to mitigate the damage. Crushed, I went to him with tears streaming down my face. "I know, grandpa," I said, laying him back down and covering him with a blanket. "I know."

An Invitation

Twenty minutes later, I came through the back door of our house on the outskirts of town and walked through the kitchen past the door to my parents' bedroom. All was dark, but, as expected, my mom and dad were waiting for me. "Did you have a good time?" my mother asked. "Yes," I mumbled quietly. "I'm going to bed." "Are you okay?" she inquired, sensing something was up. "Yes," I replied, "just tired." It was a lie. I wasn't tired, and I wasn't okay, which was becoming a bit of a theme in my life, reasserting itself at every crisis point before and after. Silently, I went to the little room I shared with my younger brother, Eric, who was fast asleep on the top bunk. I crawled, fully clothed, into the bottom bunk, leaned my back against the wall, drew my legs up to my chest and sat there reliving it all while staring into the darkness.

workplace likely contains both obsolete bureaucracy and irreplaceable institutional knowledge embedded in seemingly inefficient practices. A monthly all-hands meeting might waste productive time while building social capital no digital channel replicates. Paper backups create storage burdens yet survive server failures.

The Global Application

The practice of holding contradictions transforms how one navigates an increasingly fragmented world. Japan's lesson is not that paradox should be celebrated for its own sake, but that insisting on false coherence often destroys the very resilience that contradiction provides. Every culture operates through unresolved tensions, and recognizing this shifts engagement from judgment to genuine curiosity.

When traveling, physical or conceptual, the instinct is to resolve observed contradictions into explanatory narratives. Europeans dismiss American gun culture as irrational without examining how frontier mythology coexists with urban reality. Americans reduce French labor strikes to laziness without understanding productivity metrics that exceed their own. Japanese workplace dedication gets flattened into a workaholic caricature rather than recognized as one activated framework among several. This reductive impulse — the demand that other cultures make sense on foreign terms — prevents actual understanding.

Global citizenship begins when one stops requiring other systems to justify themselves through familiar logic. It means observing that Scandinavian social welfare coexists with some of the world's most successful startups, that Indian arranged marriages persist alongside thriving romantic love, and that Brazilian carnival's apparent chaos operates through precise neighborhood organisation by samba schools. The contradictions are not problems awaiting a solution but functional systems that have not yet been learned to read.

Professional collaboration across borders fails most often not from language barriers but from unexamined assumptions about what constitutes agreement, efficiency, or respect. A German engineer and a Japanese counterpart can speak perfect English yet entirely misunderstand each other's silences, directness, and consensus processes.

Learning to inhabit contradiction means developing code-switching fluency — not just toggling between languages but between entire frameworks of how decisions get made, relationships form, and time functions.

The deepest transformation comes from recognizing that this capacity already exists. People shift registers constantly without conscious thought: formal with authority figures, casual with peers, playful with children. They accept that scientific materialism governs professional life while maintaining friendships through emotional logic that no equation captures. They vote based on stated principles then make daily choices that contradict them. Japan simply makes visible and deliberate what other cultures perform unconsciously, offering structured permission to stop pretending life operates through a unified philosophy.

What happens to a society when it stops demanding that its competing values resolve into a single coherent narrative? Japan demonstrates the answer: it survives.

Being the Outsider

Living as a Foreigner in Japan

The System Was Not Built for You

A NATURALIZED CITIZEN OF mixed heritage walks into a Tokyo real estate office. They speak flawless Japanese, hold a stable corporate job, and possess a credit history without a single blemish. The agent takes one look at their face, notes the non-traditional name on the application, and quietly files the paperwork into a drawer where it will never be processed. The rejection has nothing to do with financial reliability. It is an administrative reflex.

This reveals Japan's deep-rooted concept of nihonjinron — the essentialist belief that Japanese identity exists as something almost biological, accessible only to those born into it. The discrimination is rarely casual prejudice; it is structural architecture. Government forms require nationality listed beside residency status. Banks demand "emergency contacts in Japan," effectively disqualifying foreign families without established networks. Apartment contracts contain foreigner clauses restricting cooking smells or noise levels that never apply to Japanese tenants.

The hāfu experience (half-Japanese individuals who are visually ambiguous to both Japanese and foreign observers) exposes this architecture most clearly. People who attended Japanese schools, speak the language natively, and hold Japanese passports still encounter the gaijin designation because their physical appearance does not match the expected template. They occupy a permanent liminal space: Japanese on paper, outsider in practice.

The hardest part of navigating this architecture is categorical separation. A foreign resident is simply gaijin — outside-person — a designation that persists regardless of language mastery, marriage to a Japanese citizen, or decades of residency. Immigration lawyers note that clients often mistake this bureaucratic immutability for personal rejection. The truth is simpler: the system was not designed to accommodate permanent integration. Understanding this distinction becomes the first step toward navigating life as a foreigner in Japan.

Strategic Positioning

Acceptance does not equal assimilation. Most integration advice conflates the two, suggesting that mastering keigo, chopstick etiquette, or precise bowing will dissolve outsider status. It will not.

What works is strategic positioning: discerning which contexts reward cultural fluency and which demand only functional competence. Understanding nemawashi — the pre-meeting consensus-building that shapes Japanese corporate decisions — proves vital for foreign professionals navigating Tokyo boardrooms. Mimicking colleagues in after-work drinking rituals, however, often breeds discomfort rather than camaraderie. Acceptance emerges where it is least expected: at neighbourhood street cleanings, where showing up consistently matters more than speaking perfectly, or at local festivals, where genuine participation outweighs linguistic precision.

The operative framework focuses on understanding where difference matters and where it does not. Formal business negotiations, temple etiquette, and interactions with older generations demand deep cultural knowledge. Other contexts simply require reliability, curiosity, and respect. The foreigners who thrive in Japan do not erase their identity; they learn to read these shifting boundaries with intelligence and grace.

Reading the Air

There is a phrase in Japanese that has no clean English equivalent: kuuki wo yomu. Literally, it means "reading the air." Functionally, it describes the ability to perceive the unspoken emotional and social atmosphere of a room and adjust one's behaviour accordingly — without being told, without asking, and without drawing attention to the act of adjustment itself.

It is the single most important social skill in Japan, and it is the one foreigners are least equipped to learn from a textbook.

Japanese children begin acquiring this skill before they can read. Elementary schools assign cleaning duties — students mop corridors, scrub toilets, sweep courtyards — not primarily for hygiene, but because shared physical labor teaches group attunement. You learn to notice when someone is struggling with their section without being asked. You learn to redistribute effort without announcing it. The lesson is not cleanliness. The lesson is peripheral awareness: the ability to sense what a group needs before the need is voiced.

By secondary school, this attunement has been refined through club activities, school trips, and the rigid social choreography of the classroom. Students learn to read a teacher's mood from posture alone, to gauge when a peer needs space versus inclusion, to understand that a slightly prolonged silence after a suggestion means the suggestion has been rejected — even if no one says so. The word chotto — technically meaning "a little" — becomes a complete vocabulary for refusal, hesitation, and discomfort, communicated entirely through tone and timing.

For foreigners, the gap is not linguistic. It is perceptual. Western communication cultures train people to make the implicit explicit: to name feelings, to state objections directly, to treat ambiguity as a problem requiring resolution. Japanese communication culture trains people to leave the implicit intact, trusting that a socially calibrated listener will receive the message without it needing to be spoken. When these two systems meet, the foreigner often reads silence as agreement, hesitation as consideration, and indirect refusal as encouragement. The misreading compounds quietly, building misunderstandings that neither party fully understands.

The practical entry point is not to master kuuki wo yomu — that takes years — but to stop filling silences. The instinct to explain, clarify, or elaborate when met with quiet is a Western reflex that consistently misfires in Japan. Silence, here, is active. It carries weight. A pause after a question often means the other person is formulating a response that preserves everyone's dignity. Interrupting that pause to rephrase the question reads as impatience, not helpfulness.

Watch how Japanese colleagues behave in meetings. Notice who speaks and when. Notice who does not speak, and whether their silence seems to carry approval or reservation. Notice whether the most senior person in the room speaks first or last — in many contexts, speaking last signals authority, not disengagement. These are not mysteries. They are a readable grammar, and like any grammar, they become legible through patient observation rather than direct instruction.

The foreigner who learns to read the air even imperfectly — who pauses before speaking, who watches before acting, who treats silence as information — will find Japan opening in ways that fluent Japanese speakers who bulldoze through social cues never experience. The country rewards attentiveness with access. That exchange is entirely available to outsiders. It simply requires learning to listen to what is not said.

The Architecture of Restraint

Japanese social interaction operates through an architecture of restraint where what remains unspoken carries more weight than what gets said aloud. Foreigners often mistake this for evasiveness, but the system functions as a precision instrument: indirection prevents confrontation, protects group cohesion, and allows face-saving exits from obligations without explicit rejection.

Wa — usually translated as harmony — demands subordinating individual preference to collective stability. This is a behavioural imperative embedded in childhood socialisation. Children learn early that deru kugi wa utareru: the nail that sticks out gets hammered down. The pressure applies universally, but foreigners feel it differently because they lack the decades of embodied conditioning that makes compliance feel natural rather than oppressive.

Tatemae and honne structure every interaction. Tatemae represents the public position, the socially acceptable stance maintained regardless of personal conviction. Honne denotes true feelings, reserved for intimate contexts where trust permits candour. A colleague's enthusiastic "Ii desu ne!" ("That's good!") about a proposal might mean genuine approval or diplomatic deflection. Distinguishing between them requires reading micro-signals: pause duration, facial tension, whether they elaborate or change subjects immediately.

This system frustrates newcomers seeking direct answers. A landlord who says "kangaete okimasu" ("I'll think about it") is declining politely. The zenzen daijōbu ("totally fine") uttered with slight hesitation often means the exact opposite. Silence functions as active communication. Rushing to fill conversational gaps violates the protocols that allow thoughtful response.

Hierarchy infuses every exchange. Status relationships determined through age, company rank, educational background, and introduction sequence dictate who bows deeper, pours drinks, speaks first,

In the wee hours of the morning, I'm not exactly sure when, I suddenly became aware of a strange, white light suspended in the air, three or four feet from my bed. Shaking my head and rubbing my eyes, I inspected it more closely. I couldn't understand where it was coming from. We lived way out in the boonies. There was no light in the room, no light coming through the window.

Curious, I got out of bed and walked around the light, and to my surprise, it intensified. I went to the window and ran my hand over every inch of the closed curtain and the light grew brighter still. Now alarmed, I jumped back into bed, pushed as far away from it as I could and started to pray. The light grew taller and changed dramatically, two shafts of light extending, one from the left and the other from the right, like two outstretched arms. That's when I heard a voice cutting through the fear, noise, and clutter in my mind. I knew instantly it was God. "Mark, I'm calling you," He said softly. I know it sounds dramatic, but that's how I heard it, over and over again. Moved to tears, I instantly jumped to the conclusion that He wanted me to be a pastor. He was fine with that assumption, I'm happy to say. "I can work with that," He might have said. But His call on my life was far more personal than that, far more invitational than vocational.

As I look back over the years, I'm amazed at how often God has come to me in moments like that — painful moments, traumatic moments, when I'm at my lowest He comes, just like He did for Hagar, Elijah, Peter and so many others. He came that night, first and foremost, to comfort me in my distress, to make me aware of His presence. I took it as something else, a dramatic call into the ministry. I received His invitation the only way I could. I was young, sleep-deprived, and emotionally disturbed. I might have missed the fullness of His invitation that night but, I'm telling you, it happened. Happy accident or not, He said, "Mark, I'm calling you" and I said, "yes," again and again, I said, "yes," until I fell asleep.

"And you want to be a pastor!"

The next morning, I went out to have breakfast. Filling a bowl with Froot Loops and milk, I looked around the table and casually announced, "I think I saw the Lord last night. He wants me to be a pastor." My mother blanched, my little brother practically snorted Froot Loops out his nose, and my big brother laughed. "W-w-what?" he shouted. "You, a pastor? You've got to be kidding." This was followed by peals of laughter and a tag team recital of my many faults and sins. If you think them unkind, you've probably never had brothers. They knew me well. Aspiring to a life in ministry, to them and all who knew me then, was ludicrous. It wasn't that I was a bad person, I just hadn't shown much interest in spiritual things. I went to church, but not by choice. I rarely read the Bible. I never filled in the blanks in the Sunday School quarterly. And my prayers were limited to a few rehearsed phrases at bedtime and the occasional cry for help. My brothers were understandably bemused. Looking back, I can hardly blame them. For at least a year thereafter, whenever I said a bad word or got angry or did something wrong, my brother's sneering rejoinder often was, "And *you* want to be a pastor!"

My parents were more circumspect. They'd always encouraged me to go to college and were excited, a year or two earlier, when I announced I wanted to be a lawyer. "Maybe you'll run for office one day or be a judge," my dad said. A lawyer in the family was something to be proud of. Lawyer jokes were not yet in vogue. But a pastor? A hired holy man? A person so heavenly minded they're no earthly good? A Bible-thumping preacher? My parents loved our pastor dearly, but it didn't stop them from critiquing his sermons on the ride home every Sunday. He often went from preaching to meddling, talking endlessly in the 1970s about the anti-Christ, the mark of the beast and Gog and Magog. It wasn't always appreciated. Shushing the raucous and irreverent incredulity of my siblings, my dad encouraged me to tell him what happened.

I took a deep breath and recounted the story in full, just like I shared it with you a moment ago. My mom was visibly shaken and a little angry hearing about the drunken escapades of her father, sorry for him and sorry for me that I had to go through that. My dad, on the other hand, sat quietly. He was waiting for the rest of the story. When I got to the part about the angel and my call to ministry, my brothers simply couldn't help themselves, sallying forth with another round of wisecracks. Ignoring them, I was watching my dad. His face fell. He could tell I was serious, that I had made up my mind, and I could see the concern in his eyes.

Lucky to have Me

Though he never voiced it, he had high hopes for me that didn't include living hand-to-mouth as a pastor. You've, no doubt, heard the phrase, "poor as church mice." I got that from my dad, alongside "we didn't have two nickels to rub together." He was born and raised in poverty, a child of the Great Depression. If, as the saying goes, they were selling ships by the seashore for five cents apiece, all he could afford to do was run up and down the dock, yelling, "Ain't that cheap?" One of nine children, he contracted rheumatic fever at age seven, spent a year in the hospital and nearly died. His mother, an ardent follower of Jesus, would visit him faithfully once a week. His father, out on the farm and also an alcoholic, never came to see him.

His long illness left his right leg six inches shorter than his left, forcing him to wear a built-up shoe for the rest of his life. When he came of age, he tried to join the military like his older brothers before him, but his disability made that impossible. Feeling sorry for him, a local juggler, of all things, wintering in my hometown, took him under his wing. My dad would eventually spend ten years traveling the country, working in the circus as a juggling clown.

I hate what horror movies have done to clowns in the last forty years, turning them all into creepy, sadistic, serial killers. My dad was known as Happy-Go-Lucky and happy he was. He was a natural showman with a showman's smile. He even appeared on *The Ted Mack Amateur Hour* in the late 1950s. Taking the juggling theme a step further, my parents met at a juggling convention and, no, I'm not making that up. My mom was engaged to another juggler when she met my father. She broke the engagement and, three months later, they were married. It was a whirlwind romance. I still tease her about it.

My brothers and I had an idyllic childhood, juggling everything from handkerchiefs and rings to clubs, knives and eventually fire. We took part in countless parades, my brothers rode unicycles and we did shows at several local churches after my dad rededicated his life to Christ in his late thirties. My parents even started a mouse circus, a curiosity with live mice that was a hit for years at county fairs and fireman's picnics all over the Tri-State area. Though the juggling wasn't ever my thing, my father had me on stage at an early age and I've always been grateful for that. We were not wealthy, not by any stretch of the imagination, but we were rich in other ways. My parents instilled a strong work ethic, encouraged independent thought, and did everything they could to help us get ahead. They wanted a better life for us. I knew that but, like the Blues Brothers, I was suddenly on a mission from God.

Whatever you may believe about dreams, visions, and angelic appearances, that first encounter, all those years ago, has sustained me through many a ministry winter. I'm grateful it happened, grateful for the way it happened, grateful to have been invited deeper into the grand story of God. Three years later, I graduated from high school and went to Bible College. Four years after that, I went to work for Jesus, convinced He was lucky to have me on his team. Thus began my long sojourn in the shallow end of the pool.

and receives deference. The sempai-kōhai system creates permanent vertical relationships: a senior from university remains a senior professionally decades later, obligating ongoing respect regardless of later career trajectories. When a foreign employee is hired laterally and promoted over a Japanese sempai, the resulting tension is not merely personal resentment. It fractures the entire team's social architecture, because the obligation structure that makes the workplace function has been violated.

Building professional trust remains complex in a system that was never designed for lateral entry.

Digital Infrastructure

Digital platforms in Japan encode cultural logic in their architecture, creating unique friction points for new arrivals. The Japanese banking and administrative system remains deeply tethered to the hanko — the personal registered seal. As these systems digitize, foreigners discover that many banking apps and municipal portals still require a digital equivalent of this seal, or demand name inputs matching their residence cards with absolute, full-width character precision. A single half-width space or a missing middle name on a digital form triggers automated rejection. The system demands absolute conformity to its established data structures. Foreign residents quickly learn that navigating Japanese digital infrastructure requires abandoning Western expectations of user-centric design in favour of mastering rigid, top-down administrative protocols.

Twitter serves as Japan's designated space for candour. Anonymity permits honne expression impossible in contexts governed by face-to-face obligation. Here, foreigners gain unexpected access. Japanese users discuss work frustrations, political opinions, and personal struggles with strangers they would never address directly at company drinking parties. The same colleague maintaining impeccable formality in meetings might candidly answer questions about mental health or immigration through anonymous threads.

Strategic use requires understanding which platforms serve which functions. Joining neighbourhood digital portal apps immediately upon moving matters more than fluency. Responding to shared community announcements even minimally is essential; silence reads as rejection. For deeper connection, Twitter and niche forums provide spaces where foreigners and Japanese exchange information without hierarchical overhead. Long-term expat communities in Tokyo, Osaka, and Kyoto use these platforms to build lateral support networks, providing the structural support that Japanese hierarchies do not extend to outsiders.

The Cognitive Shift

A two thousand and eight MIT study showed that sustained cultural immersion leads to distinct brain activation patterns in contextual processing, indicating measurable changes in pattern recognition and high-context communication. Immersive experience transforms theoretical knowledge into embodied understanding that guidebooks cannot replicate. Foreigners who commit years to Japan report a cognitive shift where cultural logic stops feeling arbitrary and starts feeling inevitable.

The silence following a colleague's sō desu ne becomes legible, distinguishing polite agreement from diplomatic refusal through micro-variations in tone and duration. The bow's angle conveys precise information about hierarchy and intent. These are not learned skills but perceptual recalibrations — the brain rewiring itself to process social cues that once seemed invisible. One stops translating and starts intuiting, reading contexts that remain opaque to short-term visitors.

The transformation runs deeper than social fluency. Long-term residents describe moments when Japanese values feel correct rather than merely understood — when waste genuinely offends, when group harmony seems rational rather than restrictive, when seasonal awareness becomes instinctive.

Exploring the Shallows

As the years went by, people would often ask me, "What would you say to someone who wants to get into the ministry?" My tongue-in-cheek reply was always the same. "Run away, run away, run away!" I was joking on the outside but on the inside, the daily grind, the constant financial difficulties, the weight of expectations, the incessant spiritual warfare, the leadership burden and the accumulated disappointment inherent in a life of Sundays, all took their toll. Why were people so unreasonable? Why the constant criticism? Why were other churches succeeding where I was failing? Why wasn't God meeting our needs? Add all of that to the pressure at home with a daughter on dialysis and you might understand my dilemma. I started feeling sorry for myself. My favorite quotes were things like, "Ministry is the only job in the world where you're shot at by the enemy in front of you and your own ranks behind you."[4] And jokes like, "Do you know why every pastor secretly wants to be an undertaker? Because when an undertaker sets them straight, they stay straight!"

Let me take you back to the Vanstone quote I mentioned earlier. He wrote, "The church is like a swimming pool in which all the noise comes from the shallow end."[5] This has been my experience. And it's not just the usual noise — read, study, pray, go, give, serve or, if you're a pastor, break this barrier, break that barrier, be relevant, be glib, be somebody — it's the expectations, the competition, the crushing weight of responsibility and so much more. That said, it's not all bad, not by a long shot. There's a lot to like about the shallow end of the pool. For example...

1. *The shallow end is where the fun begins.* I made a life there, a good life. I met my wife, raised a family, preached countless sermons, led hundreds of people to Jesus, went on missions trips, launched ministries, grew in leadership and built teams. I began my life

with God in the shallows, like we all do, grew in familiarity with Him, was baptized in the Holy Spirit and ordained for ministry. I studied the Scriptures, read countless commentaries, and learned a lot about the Bible. I don't want to disparage the shallows. The shallows are where we all get started. It's where our life with God begins. He doesn't initially invite us into the deep end of the pool. Instead, He beckons to us from the shallows and invites us to join Him there. "Come on in," He says, "the water's fine." And the water *is* fine.

2. *The shallow end is the start of something big.* You're in the pool! You've responded to Jesus. You've invited Him into your heart. He's your Savior, if not yet fully Lord, and you've been given the Holy Spirit as a lifeguard and coach. That's all good. You're in the pool of God's extravagant love, the warm water of His embrace, the cool, clear waters of His grace. It's healing water, restorative water, regenerating water, cleansing water, life-giving water, the same water that fills the deep end of the pool, only in the deep end there's more of it. You're not on the outside looking in. You're not standing on the sidelines or watching from afar. You're in! You've taken the plunge or, at least, gotten your feet wet. You may not be swimming just yet, but you're in, not out, and your decision to get in has opened a world of new possibilities. You have so much to look forward to.

3. *The shallow end is a place of discovery.* There are things I learned in the friendly confines of the shallow end of the pool that I needed to learn, experiences I needed to have, relationships I needed to cultivate, books I needed to read, places I needed to go, skills I needed to acquire and sharpen. The shallows are a great train-

Carrying Both

Living in Japan as a foreigner initiates a transformation in self-perception. The experience of permanent outsider status strips away the unspoken social fluency one once took for granted — the automatic recognition, the effortless belonging, the invisible protocols that once required no conscious thought.

Long-term foreign residents do not resolve Japan's inherent contradictions. They develop code-switching stamina, moving fluidly between cultural systems without demanding internal coherence. A conversation with someone back home explaining an internalized Japanese practice often reveals precisely how far one has travelled from their starting assumptions.

Cultural integration never reaches completion. The foreigners who thrive in Japan stop measuring success by that impossible standard.

Multiple identities are carried simultaneously. A resident bows during phone calls while their passport remains foreign. They navigate keigo hierarchies their childhood never encoded. They feel genuine affection for practices they cannot fully inherit. This is competence. The transformation is not visible in any single moment but accumulates through thousands of micro-adjustments: removing shoes without conscious thought, reading a room's emotional temperature through silence rather than speech, understanding that zenzen daijōbu means exactly the opposite of its literal translation. These adaptations do not erase the original culture; they layer new operating systems alongside existing ones, creating the code-switching fluency that defines successful long-term residence.

What is preserved matters as much as what is adapted. Maintaining aspects of an original identity — whether through language, food traditions, or communication styles — provides necessary ballast. The most culturally fluid foreigners are strategic about which elements anchor them during inevitable periods of exhaustion and alienation.

Japan does not demand a choice between integration and identity. It simply requires carrying both, activated contextually, held without resolution. What does it cost to build a life inside a system that will never fully claim you as its own?

Islands of Identity

Regional Culture and Travel

The Frontier That Remembers

HOKKAIDO'S BROWN BEARS SOMETIMES outnumber residents in remote mountain districts, revealing a fundamental truth about Japan's northernmost island. While Tokyo's core wards average around fifteen thousand seven hundred people per square kilometre, central Hokkaido's population density can drop as low as seventeen. The Daisetsuzan National Park, spanning two thousand two hundred and sixty-seven square kilometers, features vast volcanic peaks and alpine meadows where rapid weather shifts challenge multi-day treks.

This emptiness reflects a deliberate historical trajectory. Unlike Honshu's ancient agricultural terracing, Hokkaido remained largely Ainu territory until the late nineteenth century. Japan's government orchestrated systematic colonisation only after the Meiji Restoration, transforming wilderness into farmland within decades. That relatively recent settlement leaves Hokkaido with landscapes where civilisation exists as punctuation rather than paragraphs across the terrain.

The Ainu are the archipelago's original inhabitants, present for millennia before Yamato expansion northward. Their language shares no kinship with Japanese. Their spiritual world revolved around kamuy, divine beings dwelling in animals, plants, and natural forces — a cosmology entirely distinct from the religious frameworks that shaped mainland Japan.

When Tokyo established the Hokkaido Development Commission in eighteen sixty-nine, systematic erasure began. Meiji authorities banned the Ainu language in schools, seized ancestral lands for Japanese settlers, and outlawed traditional practices like iomante bear ceremonies. This was deliberate assimilation, designed to erase visible difference within a single generation. Japan did not officially recognize the Ainu as indigenous people until June two thousand and eight. Today, approximately twenty-five thousand self-identified Ainu live primarily in Hokkaido, navigating a fragile cultural revival where tourism and genuine preservation exist in uneasy tension.

The cuisine tells parallel stories. Hokkaido's celebrated seafood traditions — salmon preservation techniques, mountain vegetable foraging, fermentation methods — derive directly from Ainu knowledge systems. Modern restaurants proudly serve these dishes as "Hokkaido specialties," rarely acknowledging that their original practitioners faced systematic suppression of these very foodways under assimilation policies.

This matters because it reveals something uncomfortable about Japan's relationship with its own diversity. The nation that meticulously preserves the tea ceremony spent a century dismantling indigenous spiritual practices. Cultural variety within Japan's borders contradicts nihonjinron's foundation, exposing it as a twentieth-century construction rather than ancient truth.

The Crucible

Honshu's cultural complexity emerged from sustained collision. While Hokkaido remained a frontier and peripheral regions developed in relative remoteness, central Honshu became Japan's crucible — where competing political powers, trade routes, and religious movements converged for over a millennium.

Kyoto's location exemplifies this strategic convergence. Established as Heian-kyō in seven ninety-four precisely because mountain-ringed geography offered protection while remaining accessible to inland trade networks, the city absorbed influences from across Japan and continental Asia. Buddhist sects from Nara brought religious infrastructure, merchants from coastal ports introduced foreign goods, and samurai clans imposed military discipline — all layering atop existing Shinto shrines and agricultural communities. The result was accidental synthesis, each wave of arrivals adapting to what already existed while transforming it.

The Tōkaidō highway system formalized these intersections. Connecting Kyoto to Edo (modern Tokyo), the route's fifty-three post stations became laboratories of cultural exchange where regional dialects, culinary techniques, and craft traditions mixed continuously. Travellers carried ideas as cargo.

Culinary diversity along the Tōkaidō encoded geological and climatic realities into regional flavour. Hatcho miso from Aichi prefecture emerged from environmental necessity: humid summers demanded longer fermentation to prevent spoilage, producing a distinctively dark, bitter paste. By the eighteenth century, this adaptation became regional identity. The Nagoya cochin chicken illustrates how isolation breeds specificity. Developed in Meiji-era Aichi through selective breeding for meat density and cold resistance, the bird remained geographically contained for decades before railways distributed livestock genetics uniformly. Shizuoka's wasabi cultivation exploited mountain stream temperatures inhospitable to other crops.

These were agricultural mathematics translated into flavour.

Yet regional logic fractures under standardisation. National distribution networks homogenize ingredients that once varied prefecture by prefecture. The same Kikkoman soy sauce now appears from Hokkaido to Kyushu, erasing the subtle salinity differences coastal versus inland regions once demanded. Supermarket Hatcho miso travels to Tokyo suburbs where humid summers never required such fermentation intensity, consumed by buyers who appreciate darkness as an aesthetic rather than functional necessity.

Traditional crafts face identical tensions. Kanazawa's gold leaf beating — supplying over ninety-eight percent of Japan's decorative gold — depends on specific humidity levels the Japan Sea climate provides. Attempting replication elsewhere fails materially, not culturally. When regional specificity becomes marketing rather than constraint, the knowledge embedded in local practice — which temperature, which wood, which fermentation duration — risks preservation as performance instead of transmission as practice.

The Crossroads

Kyushu and Okinawa never fit neatly into narratives about Japanese cultural purity. Their geographic position made them Japan's frontiers — the first points of contact with continental Asia, disputed territories where empires negotiated through trade, war, and strategic marriage.

Nagasaki became Japan's sole Western window during sakoku isolation, absorbing Portuguese firearms and Dutch learning while the rest of the archipelago remained sealed. Okinawa existed as the Ryukyu Kingdom until eighteen seventy-nine, maintaining tributary relations with China while dodging complete absorption by either empire. This positioning left physical evidence everywhere. Shuri Castle's vermillion columns encoded Chinese architectural grammar foreign to Kyoto's restrained aesthetics. Nagasaki's hidden Christian communities survived two centuries of persecution by syncretising Catholic saints with Buddhist bodhisattvas — theological improvisation born from mortal necessity.

Language reveals history. In Kagoshima, arigatosaa replaces standard arigatou gozaimasu — a small shift that carries centuries of linguistic evolution. In Okinawa, basic Uchinaaguchi phrases like haisai (hello) or nifēdēbiru (thank you) acknowledge a language nearly lost to forced assimilation during the Meiji era. Speaking these words is cultural recognition.

Regional pride manifests fiercely in local flavour. Ordering okonomiyaki in Osaka and then in Hiroshima illustrates the divide. Same name, same dish in theory — but one is layered, the other mixed. One swears by soba noodles, the other by cabbage. Both are absolutely convinced they are doing it right. Department store basements (depachika) devote entire corners to meibutsu — regional specialties people gift or carry home. Whether it is Kyoto's yatsuhashi sweets, Hakata's spicy mentaiko, or Nagano's buckwheat soba, each delicacy functions as a passport to place.

The Path of Eighty-Eight

The Shikoku pilgrimage emerged in the ninth century, when Kōbō Daishi, founder of Shingon Buddhism, walked this island completing ascetic practices. His route connected eighty-eight temples across mountainous terrain, forming a one thousand two hundred kilometre circuit that embodied his teachings on enlightenment through physical and spiritual discipline. Over centuries, the path evolved from a monastic training ground to an accessible spiritual journey, open to anyone willing to walk.

The number eighty-eight carries deliberate meaning. In Buddhist numerology, it represents the eighty-eight delusions preventing enlightenment — greed, anger, ignorance multiplied across human consciousness. Each temple confronts one delusion. By visiting all eighty-eight, pilgrims symbolically purge obstacles to clarity. This framework transforms walking into meditation, where distance being ground. I have wonderful memories from my earliest days in Jesus, not to mention the three decades that followed, wonderful experiences with wonderful people — worshipping, praying, serving and dreaming big dreams. The shallows helped form my earliest understanding of who God actually is. It also helped me discover some things about myself.

4.   *The shallow end is shallow!* And that's good news. You don't begin your life with God in over your head. You wade in at your own pace — first ankle deep, then knee deep, and then, when you're ready, you might immerse yourself. There's nothing to fear. It's not too deep for comfort. Deep enough to make a difference in your life, sure, but not so deep as to alarm you. In the shallows, there's plenty of margin for error. You can always get your head above water, always get to your feet if you feel you're in danger. It doesn't take long to learn the ropes and get comfortable in the shallow end of the pool. You can plumb the depths of the shallows in no time and then gain the skills necessary to thrive there. What's more…

5.   *In the shallow end, you've got company.* Not only are you with God, you're with other believers. In fact, there's a host of others who've answered the call. Jesus told them the water was fine, and they believed Him and joined Him, just like you. Some have been enjoying the shallows for years. They know their way around, enough to offer tips and hints to help you get acclimated. You don't have to figure everything out on your own. You get to swim with others, play with others. There's a lot of excitement, energy, horseplay and camaraderie in the shallow end of the pool. You

have friends which is nothing new. You had friends before you stepped into the water. But *these* friends are more like brothers and sisters. There's always plenty of people around to help, share their experiences and give counsel. And there's safety in numbers, a sense of security. You belong!

But there's a downside to the acquisition of shallow water skills. Once you acquire them — Bible study, daily devotions, church attendance, serving, giving — you may be tempted to distinguish yourself from everyone else by studying more, praying more, serving more, going to church more and giving more. In fact, in my experience, that's the answer to almost every question, every complaint, every moment of crisis, every season of desolation in the shallow end of the pool. Are you having a problem in your marriage? "You need to study more, pray more, go to church more, serve more and give more." Are you struggling with depression? "You need to study more, pray more, go to church more, serve more and give more." Are you worried about the future? Again, "Study more, pray more, go to church more, serve more and give more." These are often the only answers in the shallows. The road to transformation, I came to believe, leads exclusively through behavioral modification. You just need to try harder, sacrifice more, get serious about your faith.

But for all my trying, striving, and sacrificing, I was regularly failing. I'd hold the line for a week or two — praying, confessing, writing in my journal, even fasting — then crash and burn, stumbling and bumbling my way into a long season of spiritual inactivity, regret, self-recrimination and despair. "Couldn't you keep watch with me for one hour?" I'd hear Jesus say on repeat in my head, a favorite device of the enemy to keep me wallowing in shame. "I have so much to do that I shall spend the first three hours in prayer,"[6] I'd hear Martin Luther say and, again, I'd feel the weight of my inadequacy, my inability to step up, measure up and keep up while fighting the urge to tell Martin Luther to shut up. Weeks would go by, sometimes months, before I'd find the intestinal fortitude to strap it all back on again, like a seventy-pound rucksack, and take up the hopeful refrain of *The Little Engine that Could*, "I think I can, I think I can, I think I can," knowing that I probably couldn't. After nearly thirty years of ministry, trying so hard to obey and live up to God's call on my life, I felt no closer to God. I was on a hyper-spiritual, I-serve-Jesus-how-about-you treadmill of performance, held captive by a growing list of shoulds and oughts and a desperate need to prove myself. I was weary in well doing. In truth, I felt like a lonely automaton, simply going through the motions. And it wasn't the first time. I'd reached this same crisis point many times over the years — depressed, disillusioned, ready to quit and questioning, always questioning, "Is this all there is? Is this what it's really all about?"

Life Beyond the Buoys

Despite my despair and the seemingly endless, white-knuckle cycle of try, achieve, stumble, fail, wallow, and repeat, I held out hope that there might yet be something more, something I'd yet to discover, a life with God apart from all the noise. What might await me, I wondered, beyond the foreboding string of blue and white buoys that marked the spot where the shallows end and the deep begins? I'd read countless biographies of celebrated Christians who described an intimacy with God I'd never experienced, a familiarity I'd never known. And I told myself, for years, that they were special, super Christians, not normal like the rest of us. But I couldn't help but wonder, "What if I'm wrong? What if there's more?" After all, Jesus Himself said,

> "Are you tired? Worn out? Burned out on religion? Come to me.
> Get away with me and you'll recover your life. I'll show you how
> to take a real rest. Walk with me and work with me — watch how

I do it. Learn the unforced rhythms of grace. I won't lay anything heavy or ill-fitting on you. Keep company with me and you'll learn to live freely and lightly (Matthew 11:28-30 MSG)."

"Yes!" I cried out to God that day in my office, stumbling for the umpteenth time under a load I thought I had to carry. "I'm tired. I'm worn out. I'm burned out on religion." "Well, then," I thought I heard Him say, "come to me. Get away with me and you'll recover your life." I'm happy to say that I did and I have. Would you like to recover your life? You can. I'm here to tell you, you can. It's all possible, everything Jesus promised us. I mean, think about it. What would it be like to be with God without always having to do for God? What would it be like to trade duty and obligation for a life lived in response to God's invitations? What would it be like to experience God's presence beyond just believing He exists? What would it be like to not just know God loves you, but to actually feel loved by God? What would it be like to let go of all the roles, titles, and achievements that have been a source of identity, worth and value for you apart from who you are in Christ and live out of your true identity, who God says you are? What would it be like to live freely and lightly?

What I'm about to share with you is my story. It's the story of how God led me out of the all-too-familiar shallows and what I learned in the process. It's my story, my journey, and I have a long way to go. Your journey will, no doubt, be different, but it is our stories that connect us. I'll share mine with you hoping, one day, in this life or the next, you'll share yours with me. It all began with a paradigm shift, followed by a series of discoveries. First, the paradigm shift. Something needed to change. I needed to stop merely trying and start training.

two

Training, Not Just Trying

*"Everyone who hears these words of mine and puts them into practice
is like a wise man who built his house on the rock."*
~ Matthew 7:24

*"In a culture that craves the big, the entertaining, the dramatic,
and the shocking (sometimes literally), cultivating a life with space for
silence and repetition is necessary for sustaining a life of faith."* [7]
~ Tish Harrison Warren

"**P**lay a twenty-four-hour tennis marathon!" they said. "It'll be fun!"
"Hmmm," I replied skeptically. It was sadly the best of several
bad ideas and, in retrospect, I should have known better, but as the newly
minted president of the junior class, I was responsible for raising money
for the junior-senior banquet. I don't remember how much money exactly,
but at the time, it seemed like a small fortune. "What else can we do?"
asked one of my friends pleadingly. "Yes," I thought to myself, shaking

my head in despair, "what else *can* we do?" I was carrying a full load of classes while working a part-time job as a tennis instructor on campus. I simply didn't have the bandwidth nor could I envision myself organizing an endless series of nickel-and-dime fundraisers over the course of the year, hoping it would be enough. The twenty-four-hour tennis marathon seemed like the perfect solution.

Starting at 4pm on a Friday afternoon, I would play twenty-four consecutive hours of tennis against twenty-four different opponents with five-minute breaks each hour. My crew of friends and fellow class officers would canvas the campus, two weeks before the event, begging students and professors alike to pledge so much per hour. It was slow going. One week into the pledge cycle, we were nowhere near our goal. No one seemed to care, so we made it an all-or-nothing proposition. If I made it twenty-four consecutive hours without quitting, folks had to pay what they pledged. If I didn't, they owed nothing. It was a masterstroke of marketing, just what we needed to push us over the top. Frankly, I was amazed, and a little put out, by how many people were suddenly willing to bet against me.

As the pledges came pouring in, I started "training" with my friend, Steve. I put the word "training" in quotes, just now, because, even then, I knew whatever we did it wouldn't be enough. I mean, how does one train to play twenty-four straight hours of tennis in a couple of weeks? The notion was absurd, a prescription for pain with my signature at the bottom. Nevertheless, after a solid five minutes of deliberation, we decided to run five miles a night while I carried a heavy lead pipe hoping against hope it would help me build additional arm strength. That's it! That was our whole plan! Running around campus for two weeks with a lead pipe in my hand. I might as well have been training for a part as a street thug in West Side Story for all the good it did. I was trying, not training and it showed.

"How did I do?" you ask. I started well enough. In fact, for the first few hours, I was on fire, fueled by a crowd that had come from miles around to watch me fall apart. But, when night fell, the euphoria of the fast start quickly faded as I was left alone on the court, hour after hour, with a fresh new opponent and a couple of sleep-deprived friends for comfort. At midnight, six hours into the marathon, I was a limp dishrag, dead on my feet, barely able to keep the ball in play. At four in the morning, the halfway mark, I couldn't remember who I was or why I was doing this. This was the moment, in the dead of night, when a real athlete might have "trusted their training" but I hadn't been training, not really, not for long. As the sun came up, I stumbled along on fumes. Every fifty-five-minute period seemed an eternity, every five-minute break but a few seconds. I was tired, sure, but I'd been tired before. I was a twenty-year-old college student who was used to the lack of sleep. Like millions of college students, before and after, I routinely pulled an all-nighter whenever it suited me. That was easy. This was something else. I hurt in places I had never hurt before.

Now, I'd like to tell you that the thought of quitting never entered my mind. I'd *really* like to tell you that. You probably weren't there and even if you were, it's so long ago, you probably don't remember. I could easily employ a little harmless, revisionist history here painting myself as a shining example of courage and determination in the face of adversity and who's to know? But it simply isn't true. I made it to the eighteenth hour on nothing but adrenaline because I knew that that was the hour Dianne Hotalen had agreed to serve as a ball girl. There you have it! The truth finally comes out. For me, it was all about a girl, always about a girl and not just any girl! I'd been wanting to meet her for more than a month, looking for the right opportunity, and my friend, Chris, did me a solid and set it up. I was living for that eighteenth hour, determined to finally make her acquaintance.

When she arrived, I swear the heaven's opened, and I heard choirs of angels, but I might have been hallucinating. I wasn't exactly at my best. By that time, I'd been awake and on my feet for a day and a half. I'd mostly stumbled and bumbled forward and backward, side-to-side, for several miles, logging thousands of steps, which wasn't even a thing back then. I'd also hit several thousand tennis balls, making just enough contact to barely get it over the net. I literally had nothing left. I was gassed, knackered, shattered, as the Brits might say. The fire that burned so brightly in the beginning was now nothing more than a smoldering wick. Suddenly, none of that mattered. I introduced myself to Dianne and as we engaged in our first conversation, the first of many thousands of conversations to follow, I was immediately rejuvenated — running, jumping and swinging from the heels at every ball like a hyperactive squirrel on Red Bull.

That hour with her, talking between points, was the shortest hour in a day full of hours that stretched out endlessly like Frodo's trip to Mordor. It was over far too soon. "I didn't even get her number," I thought to myself five minutes after she left, but it didn't matter. It was a small campus and I probably wouldn't have been able to write it down anyway. By the end of the marathon, I could barely grip the racket with either hand. My left shoulder had swollen to the size of a grapefruit and was so painful it would require multiple cortisone injections and three weeks with my arm in a sling to recover. My right shoulder hadn't fared much better as I'd played several hours with my right arm, happy to be somewhat ambidextrous. Just making contact with the ball in those final, agonizing hours was enough to nearly bring me to my knees. Nevertheless, I had met "the companion of my future life," to quote Jane Austen, and for that I will always be grateful. But I also got a painful lesson in the need for proper training.

There Is No Try

Let's put the finishing touches on that Vanstone quote. He wrote,

> "The church is like a swimming pool in which all the noise comes
> from the shallow end. But most of the wisdom is to be found in
> the deep end, among those who have taken the time to cultivate

the habits and disciplines to learn to swim in deeper waters. If we are to love God with all our heart, soul, mind and strength, then we need the kind of sustained learning that leads us into the deep end of the pool."[8]

When I first read that, many years ago, I knew, in my heart, it was true. There *is* wisdom in the shallow end of the pool, no doubt about it. But that wisdom is in limited supply, adequate only to aid and sustain life in the shallows. If you want something more, what the Apostle James called "wisdom from above,"[9] you have to go deeper. You have to take the time to cultivate the habits and disciplines that will enable you to swim in deeper waters. This I hadn't done. I hadn't taken the time. I lacked spiritual discipline. Even after thirty years of ministry, my life with God, if you could call it that, was mostly spits and starts. I'd buy the latest devotional, start a new Bible reading plan, write a few pages in a fresh, leather-bound journal or adopt a new prayer model only to give it up a few days later. I constantly felt like a failure. I felt like a failure because I had come to regard spiritual disciplines or practices as an end in themselves, the proof of an intimate relationship with Jesus, when they are not the end but a means to a deeper, more satisfying, life with God. Something needed to change. I needed to pivot, as they say, to plant my foot in the ground and, by the grace of God, turn away from a trying life and start training.

In desperation, and true to form, I decided to "try" the *Ignatian Exercises*. Here, again, was the root of my problem. If you know anything about the *Exercises of Ignatius of Loyola*, you know they aren't for trying, but for training. One does not "try" the *Ignatian Exercises*. You either "do or do not. There is no try,"[10] to quote Yoda, who understood that much, though he lacked a biblical worldview. Besides, desperation is no time for trying. Frustration, desolation, and despair are no time for trying. You need to start training. Training is what's needed. It's what I needed.

Enter Ignatius

Have you ever heard of Ignatius of Loyola? I knew the name, but nothing more. I had certainly never heard of the spiritual exercises he developed in the 1500s as a tool for discipleship. Yet, suddenly, there I was at a conference and a very successful pastor that I'd known and admired for years was talking about his experience with the *Exercises*, how it's all rooted in Scripture with an emphasis on the life, death, and resurrection of Jesus Christ and all that he did for us. Seeing how deeply affected he was really got my attention. In the end, he recommended a book, a Protestant approach to the Spiritual Exercises of Saint Ignatius by Larry Warner, entitled *Journey with Jesus*. Intrigued, I bought the book and took it on a prayer retreat a couple of months later. That prayer retreat marked one of the lowest moments of my life in ministry. I was so exhausted I slept through the first full day and part of the night. I had all but decided I was done as a pastor and I didn't want to talk with God about it. I didn't mind talking *to* Him, but I didn't want to talk *with* Him. I didn't want Him changing my mind.

As I read the first chapter, I felt dead inside. I don't know how else to describe it. It was talking about things I'd never heard of, much less employed — Lectio Divina, imaginative prayer, the daily examen. It was all so unfamiliar to me. "Is this something a Christian should even do?" I wondered. "Is this Catholic? New Age? Is it even orthodox?" Then I read, "The goal is to encounter God through His living Word rather than merely learn [more] about God."[11] I wanted that. I wanted to encounter God, but I had doubts, doubts about the practices, yes, but more to the point, I doubted myself. In this season of my life, I couldn't maintain a regular devotional life. How was I going to engage with God in all these unfamiliar ways every single day for the next nine months? Then, at the beginning of chapter 2, the author gave me an out, permission to stop and go no further. He wrote, "Ignatius created the Spiritual Exercises with the intention that a spiritual director would be involved."[12] That was all I needed to hear. Relieved, I thought, "I don't have a spiritual director." In truth, I didn't even know what that was exactly but, whatever it was, I knew I didn't have one. I sighed, closed the book, and picked up my iPad. It was time, once again, to play SimCity and escape into my own little world, a world built to my exact specifications — two and a half million people in a city by the sea, served by a single church, pastored by me.

A little while later, my daughter, Alexis, started meeting with a spiritual director and, as she shared her experience, setting aside time regularly to talk with someone about her walk with God, I saw a dramatic change in her life. My wife, Dianne, then began training to become a spiritual director, drawn more to the opportunity to walk in community with others while pursuing a deeper life with God. As she progressed through the training and began meeting with a spiritual director herself, she helped me better understand what a spiritual director does. The word "director" is a little misleading. My spiritual director has never been directive. On the contrary, he listens, reflects, encourages, highlights what God might be doing and helps me remember where I was so I can see how far I've come. He's more like a spiritual listener, companion, or friend. Over the years, knowing I was going to meet with my spiritual director at a set time each month has helped me stay motivated in my walk with God. And the *Exercises* helped me finally develop some consistent spiritual habits — silence and solitude, prayerful reflection, contemplation and self-examination — while I learned how to meditate on and encounter God in Scripture.

Full disclosure, my nine-month journey through the *Ignatian Exercises* took eighteen months, not because I was lazy, though I struggled at first to keep up, but mostly because I was so overwhelmed by what I was learning I had to slow down to take it all in. I had never walked with Jesus for so concentrated a time, with Him every day like one of His disciples, following Him to the cross and beyond. It was like drinking from a fire hose, all that God was showing me about Himself, myself and others. I cried and journaled. I took long walks with God, something I had never done before.

I began to see God in nature, in a good meal shared with family, in a job well done, in the laughter of those around me. I sat in silence, and for the first time, simply enjoyed being with Him.

Are the *Ignatian Exercises* for everyone? I think you need to be called to them, to feel drawn to them, sensing God's invitation. I also think it's important to pay attention to the season you're in. Is this the best tool for this season of your life? And make no mistake, the *Exercises* are merely a tool, a daily prayer practice, nothing more. They're not "magical," in and of themselves, or the cure for a flagging devotional life or the missing ingredient to a troubled marriage or a shortcut to a deeper life with God. There are no shortcuts to a deeper life with God. If you do the *Exercises* just to do them and say that you have, you'll get from the experience precisely what you're willing to invest, nothing more. It will not be transformative, not in any meaningful way. I want to say this as clearly as I can. Doing the *Ignatian Exercises* does not guarantee you passage out of the shallow end of the pool. It's like anything else people do that a lot of other people are doing. Your motives matter. "Past experience," as the saying goes, or the positive experience of others, "is not indicative of future results." I've known people who completed the *Ignatian Exercises* and came away unchanged, unmoved, no closer to God than they were before. It's a tool, my friends, and as a tool, its value is not in what it can do but how you use it. If you use it as a means to a deeper, more intimate love relationship with Jesus, if that is what you want more than anything else, God will help you find it. He wants it more than you do. You will go deeper if you take the time to practice your faith regardless of the tools you use.

Practice, Practice, Practice

In my early fifties, my desire for more of God finally overcame my reticence or, more honestly, my fear. I wanted to go deeper and for that, as I've said, I needed deep water skills. So, I entered a time of sustained learning, as Vanstone suggests. My search for the more led me to the *Ignatian Exercises* and my experience with the *Exercises*, those eighteen months, sent my life in a whole new direction. I went from puttering with the things of God to practicing the presence of God, from chafing under the guilt, pressure and heaviness of a performance-oriented life to resting in His love. If that's what you want, if that's what you're looking for, if you want the easy yoke and the light burden Jesus offers you, if you want peace regardless of your circumstances, if you want to be rooted and grounded in love, you have to practice your faith.

Jesus Himself encouraged us to practice. He said, "Everyone who hears these words of mine and puts them into *practice* is like a wise man who built his house on the rock (Matthew 7:24)." He said, "My mother and brothers are those who hear God's word and put it into *practice* (Luke 8:21)." He warned the religious elite of His day, saying, "Woe to you Pharisees, because you give God a tenth…but you neglect justice and the love of God. You should have *practiced* the latter without leaving the former undone (Luke 11:42)." Practice, practice, practice. The Apostle Paul picks up on the theme in Romans 12. He writes, "Share with the Lord's people who are in need. *Practice* hospitality (Romans 12:13)." And, "Whatever you have learned or received or heard from me, or seen in me — put it into *practice*. And the God of peace will be with you (Philippians 4:9)." You've probably heard, "practice makes perfect" but I like "practice makes permanent" or "practice makes progress." I'm not sure where I heard those, but they better reflect my life experience.

This idea of practicing the faith is rooted in first-century Judaism. As Lauren Winner wrote, "Practice is to Judaism what belief is to Christianity. That is not to say that Judaism doesn't have doctrine or dogma. It is rather to say that for Jews, the essence of the thing is in the doing, action. Your faith might come and go but your practice ought not waver. In fact, Judaism suggests that the repeating of a practice is the best way to ensure that a doubter's faith will return."[13] We were meant to practice, to be doers of the Word, as James wrote, not hearers only.[14] This is where spiritual disciplines come in. And I know that's not a popular word, *discipline*. But where do you think we got the word *disciple*? A disciple is simply a practicing follower of Jesus, someone who's both hearing *and* doing (James 1:22).

I'm not offended by the word *discipline*. I often use the words *'disciplines'* and *'practices'* interchangeably. They mean much the same thing. Author James Bryan Smith prefers to call them "soul-training exercises." I like that even better. He writes, "Spiritual disciplines are actually not 'spiritual' at all. Thinking they are 'spiritual' leads people to practice them as isolated activities that are done to make a person more 'spiritual,' whatever that means. They are done with no specific aim and are often done legalistically to gain the favor of God or others."[15] And he's right. We often turn altars into idols, elevating the practices above the presence of God, glorying in our practices as some kind of proof of eternal life when they are merely the means to a deeper, more intimate love relationship with Jesus. "The ancient [spiritual] disciplines form us to respond to God, over and over always, in gratitude, in obedience, and in faith."[16] We draw near, we are changed, we learn to respond to God as we practice.

And I'm not talking about simply doing what you've always done more earnestly or more often — read more, pray more, go to church more, give more, serve more. I'm talking about adding some new tools to your toolbox, engaging God in ever-deepening ways. I'm talking about moving from reading Scripture to meditating on Scripture, from one-sided, wordy prayers to abiding or listening prayer, from semi-regular church attendance to engaging in loving community, from tithing to sacrificial giving, from loving others to loving your enemy. If you do what you've always done, you'll get what you've always gotten and you'll go no deeper. You need deep-water skills, soul-training exercises that will help you grow in intimacy with God.

Training, Not Just Trying

As I've mentioned, I was living a trying life, double entendre intended. I was trying to follow Jesus, trying to maintain a daily time with God, trying to read through the Bible in a year, trying to pray for others and pray the Psalms and journal and go on an annual prayer retreat — all the things everyone, including me, said you should do and it all ended in a kind of manic, unsatisfying desperation. Trying and, more often than not, failing is exhausting. I had had enough of trying. I needed to start training. As the Apostle Paul wrote, "Do you not know that in a race all the runners run, but only one gets the prize? Run in such a way as to get the prize. Everyone who competes in the games goes into *strict training*. They do it to get a crown that will not last, but *we do it* to get a crown that will last forever. Therefore I do not run like someone running aimlessly; I do not fight like a boxer beating the air. No, I strike a blow to my body and make it my slave so that after I have preached to others, I myself will not be disqualified for the prize (1 Corinthians 9:24-27)."

He's advocating for training over trying, using sports metaphors. Natural talent aside, the difference between me and a professional golfer is the difference between training and trying. The difference between my body and Dwayne Johnson's body is the difference between training and… not really trying. If you want to do anything in the physical realm — climb a mountain, run a marathon, or learn how to juggle — you have to do more than try. You have to train. What does it mean to train? I love John Ortberg's definition. He said, "To train means arranging your life around those practices that enable you to do what you cannot now do by direct effort."[17] The point of training in sports is to get stronger, to improve your performance, so you arrange your life around practices through which you gain the ability to do what you cannot now do. Training and practice go hand-in-hand. Training involves practice. The point of our training as believers is to become more like Jesus by the power of the Holy Spirit and grow closer to God in the process. How do we make progress toward these goals? We have to arrange our lives around those practices that help us cooperate with the Holy Spirit in our own transformation. The practices themselves don't change us. God does the changing, but practices like abiding prayer and meditating on Scripture help us be available to God.

In an effort to reawaken a significant portion of her childhood, growing up as a missionary kid in West Africa, my wife, Dianne, has been practicing French, the beautiful language of her youth. In a very real way, she's in training — working diligently to expand her vocabulary, improve her accent and find a new level of fluency and functionality in the language. I've watched as she has literally rearranged her life around the practices necessary to enable her to do what she was heretofore unable to do by direct effort. She's not yet fluent in the language, nor is that the goal, but she's making progress. I also want to learn French but, unlike my wife, I am unwilling to rearrange my life and practice. What I do, instead, is make up faux-French words, speak in an exaggerated faux-French accent, I use the word *faux* a lot and answer every question she puts to me in French with a rousing, "Oui, madam" or "Oh, oui, mon Chéri." The difference between my accent and Dianne's accent, my "French" and her French is the difference between training and pretending. She's speaking French. I'm imitating Pepé Le Pew.

When it comes to following Jesus, so many are trying when they should be training. Transformation, on any level, involves training. We know that. We know it intuitively. Now, it's at this point, when we're determined to move from trying to training, that we often get overwhelmed. So much needs to change. So many of our thoughts and attitudes and habits need attention. There are things we need to discover about ourselves, things we may not even be aware of — roadblocks and obstacles that have stood in the way of our growth, impeding our progress along the path maybe for comes spiritual progress measured in footsteps rather than abstractions.

Traditional pilgrims wore white — the colour of death. The white vest (hakui) and conical hat (sugegasa) signalled a pilgrim's willingness to die on the path, surrendering ego before beginning. The morbid origins of the costume have faded from common knowledge, but the costume itself has not. Modern walkers still adopt this uniform, and wearing it triggers osettai — a practice where locals offer food, lodging, or money to pilgrims. This hospitality reflects merit-making; supporting pilgrims earns spiritual credit equivalent to walking oneself.

Today's pilgrims walk for reasons Kōbō Daishi never anticipated. Germans seeking clarity after divorce, Taiwanese students questioning career paths, Americans processing grief. They complete sections over years, returning annually to walk another hundred kilometers. Some never finish. The incompleteness itself becomes the point.

The route has adapted to logistical realities that ensure its survival. Buses connect temples for elderly pilgrims whose knees will not carry them up mountain passes. Smartphone apps track temple stamps and locate the next lodging. Yet osettai persists — elderly women still press onigiri into pilgrims' hands at bus stops.

The Architecture of Care

Omotenashi is often translated as hospitality, but the word misses the operational mechanism. It is the art of invisible care — anticipating what someone needs before they ask, offering something with no expectation of return.

A taxi driver adjusts the seat heater before a passenger realizes they are cold. An innkeeper leaves a handwritten weather forecast with a breakfast tray. A bowed head and a soft "arigatou" lands with more care than ceremony. In a Kyoto ryokan, seasonal flowers arranged in a room are not chosen at random, but timed to match the exact week of the year. In Tohoku, a neighbor offers freshly picked apples without a word. In Okinawa, a family invites a lost stranger in for lunch and refuses payment.

What makes omotenashi powerful is its lack of performance. It is not branding or customer service protocol. People do not think of it as something extra; they treat it as the baseline. Some of the most profound experiences happen in places with no curated charm — a cup of tea placed by an elbow, a path swept clean before a walk. Gestures that say: We saw you coming, and you are welcome here.

The Logic of Wandering

Traveling in Japan possesses a particular rhythm — not a checklist, but a quiet choreography that rewards attention rather than demanding it. A train is not just transit; it is an observation deck where tiled rooftops flicker past, mountains rise in the distance, and fields glow golden with the season. The silence between stops functions as part of the journey.

The infrastructure supports stillness as much as movement. The trains run on time, but the deepest understanding occurs when one gets off at the wrong stop. Renting a bicycle in the countryside. Hiking a stretch of the old Tōkaidō Road. Following the scent of incense to an unfamiliar temple tucked between modern buildings. A path behind a shrine leading into cedar woods. A small-town station smelling of soy sauce and firewood. A local festival discovered by chance, where children carry lanterns through dusk.

In areas like Niigata Prefecture, within the Echigo-Tsumari Art Triennale, abandoned elementary schools have faced obsolescence due to rural depopulation. Instead of demolition, they have been revitalized through art initiatives. Kilns fire in gymnasiums; looms occupy staff rooms. Traditional crafts find new life through contemporary methods. Elderly villagers teach visiting artists regional pottery glazing methods passed down through generations, while those same artists introduce digital pattern-making software to transform historical textile designs. The exchange flows both ways, creating something neither purely traditional nor entirely modern, but deeply resonant with the region's evolving identity.

A culture thrives when it stops trying to preserve its past in amber and instead allows it to breathe, adapt, and rewrite itself in the hands of whoever arrives next.

Moving Through Japan

The Speed of Trust

THE FIRST SHINKANSEN LEFT Tokyo for Osaka on October first, nineteen sixty-four, nine days before the Olympics opening ceremony. It reached a maximum speed of two hundred and ten kilometres per hour, cutting the previous travel time in half. That initial five hundred and fifteen kilometre line was a declaration that a nation flattened nineteen years earlier could now move faster than anywhere else on Earth.

Today's network spans two thousand nine hundred and fifty-one kilometres. The Nozomi reaches two hundred and eighty-five kilometres per hour on the Tōkaidō route. The average delay is eighteen seconds. Not eighteen minutes — seconds.

This precision is not accidental, and it is not merely technical. Trains undergo seven-minute cleaning rotations between arrivals. Platform markings guide passengers to exact door locations. Conductors bow upon entering each car, even when no one is watching. These are not efficiency protocols — they are the same values that appear in the tea ceremony, the omakase counter, and the neighborhood street cleaning: the belief that doing something well, every time, without exception, is itself a form of respect. The Shinkansen does not just move people quickly. It demonstrates what a society looks like when collective trust is treated as infrastructure.

Precision Archaeology

Tokyo's rail system reveals something most visitors misread at first glance. What seems like chaos is actually precision archaeology — three distinct rail networks operating simultaneously, each layer preserving the logic of a different era.

JR lines form the structural skeleton. The Yamanote loop circles central Tokyo in sixty minutes, linking Shinjuku, Shibuya, Tokyo Station, and every major node between. These are Japan Railways' domain: the green trains, the overhead passes, the long-distance connections radiating outward. JR owns the connective tissue of the city.

Private railways tell a different story. Companies like Odakyu, Keio, and Tokyu built entire suburbs, then connected them to the city centre. This vertical integration explains why massive department stores crown terminal stations. A passenger is not merely riding Tokyu's train; they are entering Tokyu's commercial universe, designed from bedroom community to shopping destination.

Metro lines burrow beneath everything else. Thirteen lines operated by two separate entities — Tokyo Metro and Toei — weave through the underground with fare systems that do not always speak to each other. Transferring between operators often means exiting one gate, navigating corridors, and paying again.

The deeper point is what this layered complexity reveals about how Japan handles change. The century-old solutions still operate because they still solve real problems. Nothing was demolished to make way for something newer and cleaner. Each system was built around what existed, not instead of it. Tokyo's rail network is kaizen made physical — continuous improvement that accumulates rather than replaces.

Local Fluency

Buses demand a different literacy than trains. While rail networks broadcast their logic through multilingual signs and color-coded apps, buses assume local fluency. Route maps compress kanji characters into dense grids. Announcements roll past in Japanese. The fare system shifts by city: Tokyo charges a flat rate regardless of distance, while Kyoto calculates fares through numbered zones displayed above the driver's seat.

In most cities, passengers board through the rear door and take a numbered ticket. When exiting, they match that number to the illuminated fare board and pay accordingly. Some regions reverse the entire process, requiring front-door boarding and immediate payment.

Taxis operate through their own visual language. A red light in the lower windshield signals availability; green means occupied. The rear door opens automatically — the driver controls it remotely, so passengers should never reach for the handle. Drivers wear white gloves. Vehicles are immaculate. Card readers appear inconsistently outside Tokyo and Osaka, so carrying cash remains wise. Japan's addressing system does not follow Western grids, making a destination shown on a phone screen far more effective than attempting pronunciation.

The white gloves are worth pausing on. They are not a uniform requirement in any formal sense. They are a choice — a small, visible signal that the person behind the wheel considers this work worth doing with care. It is the same instinct that produces the folded triangle at the end of a hotel toilet roll, the two-handed receipt at a convenience store, the bow at an empty train car. Omotenashi does not switch off when the tourist is not looking.

The Economics of Distance

Beneath the sleek surface of bullet trains lies a patchwork of regional deals, budget carriers, and unspoken strategies that reward the traveller who plans with intention.

For long-distance travellers, the Japan Rail Pass functions as a passport to the Shinkansen network. Available only to foreign tourists, it offers unlimited rides on most JR trains for a set period of seven, fourteen, or twenty-one days. A single round-trip from Tokyo to Kyoto nearly pays for a seven-day pass. It requires purchasing before entering Japan, or online at a premium once inside, and only makes financial sense if the itinerary includes multiple long trips within its validity period.

Regional rail passes offered by the various JR companies cater to more localized travel. The Kansai Area Pass covers unlimited JR rides across Osaka, Kyoto, Nara, and Kobe for a fraction of the full JR Pass price. Many of these local passes include Shinkansen-lite services and buses, making them well-suited to focused itineraries.

Japan's long-distance highway buses are a budget traveller's best resource. Companies like Willer Express and JR Bus offer clean, comfortable overnight rides between cities, often costing a tenth of the equivalent train fare. The journey takes longer, but saves on both transport and a night's accommodation.

Domestic flights offer another alternative. Low-cost carriers — Peach Aviation, Jetstar Japan, and Skymark — operate routes across Japan, and flying can be cheaper than the train for long hauls to Hokkaido or Okinawa. Booking in advance is necessary, and baggage policies are strict, but the time saved is real.

The Digital Key

IC cards — Suica, PASMO, ICOCA — function as universal access keys across Japan's transport infrastructure.

These rechargeable smart cards eliminate the constant mental arithmetic of distance-based pricing: tap on entry, tap on exit, and fare calculation happens invisibly.

They work seamlessly across rail companies that remain technically incompatible, regional boundaries that once demanded separate tickets, and transport modes that previously required navigating different payment systems.

The adoption rate exceeds ninety percent in major cities. Tourists can purchase them at any major station within minutes, loading value at vending machines that default to English interfaces. They serve as payment for local transportation — subways, buses, trams — and at convenience stores, vending machines, and many restaurants.

Mobile apps extend this logic into comprehensive journey planning. Google Maps provides routing with high accuracy, displaying platform numbers and precise transfer walking times. The NAVITIME Japan Transit app calculates multi-leg journeys accounting for train types, connections, and JR Pass optimisation. Japan Transit Planner filters routes by cost versus speed, exposing tradeoffs that transform navigation from guesswork into informed choice.

Staying connected requires planning. While some stations and cafés offer free WiFi, the signal is inconsistent and logging in often requires digital registration. Renting a pocket WiFi device or purchasing a local SIM card at the airport provides reliable coverage when navigating Kyoto's grid or finding the correct exit in Shinjuku Station. Voice-Tra offers smooth spoken translation, useful when explaining dietary needs or asking directions in a smaller town.

Japan's transport network is, in the end, a portrait of the country's values made functional. The precision is not performance. The cleanliness is not for tourists. The bowing conductor and the seven-minute cleaning rotation and the eighteen-second average delay all emerge from the same source: a collective agreement, renewed daily, that the way a thing is done matters as much as whether it gets done at all. Traveling through Japan is not just a matter of getting from one place to another. It is a sustained lesson in what a society looks like when it takes that agreement seriously.

Chapter Seventeen

Traveling as a Guest

The Language of Subtlety

JAPANESE COMMUNICATION DOES NOT operate like English mistranslated. It is an entirely different system where directness signals social failure.

When a colleague says zenzen daijōbu ("totally fine"), context determines whether they mean genuine agreement or polite refusal. The phrase stays identical. What shifts is barely perceptible: a slight hesitation before speaking, breath pattern, whether they meet your eyes.

Native speakers absorb these signals through years of calibration.

This is structural necessity, not evasiveness. The keigo honorific system encodes hierarchy directly into verb conjugation, making egalitarian speech grammatically impossible. Every sentence requires calculating status, adjusting formality across five levels from casual to supremely polite. Incorrect verb endings create social offence by misidentifying relationships.

Silence functions as active communication. A ten-second pause during meetings signals disagreement more clearly than verbal objection. Physical gestures carry equal precision: fifteen-degree bows acknowledge acquaintances, thirty degrees show respect, forty-five degrees apologize seriously.

What appears opaque becomes legible once the foundational principle is accepted: meaning resides in implication, not statement.

Purity and Architecture

At Fushimi Inari shrine, visitors wearing outdoor shoes step directly onto tatami mats, unaware they have violated an ancient boundary. Staff intervene quietly. The moment passes without confrontation, but the breach has already happened.

Shoes encode purity logic inherited from Shinto tradition. Outdoor footwear carries contamination from public space; interior zones demand separation. This is a functional distinction between polluted and purified ground, manifested in physical architecture.

Restaurants provide plastic bins at entrances. Ryokan feature genkan entryways with visible floor-level changes. Temple grounds display organized shoe racks. The system operates through environmental cues, not posted instructions. Japanese visitors remove shoes reflexively, positioning them outward for easy retrieval, switching to provided slippers where designated.

The principle scales beyond footwear. Photographing strangers without permission violates privacy. Eating while walking through residential neighborhoods signals disrespect. Phone conversations on trains break the communal silence. None require language fluency; they demand observation, demonstrating attentiveness to systems millions navigate daily without conscious thought.

The Rhythms of Restraint

Kehai — anticipatory awareness — means reading spatial temperature before entering. Crowded trains demand backpack removal to front-carry position. Loud conversations cease once doors close. These are observable rhythms requiring only attention.

Minimal-impact presence is the goal. Holding bags close rather than swinging freely. Stepping aside before stopping to check phones. Waiting for train passengers to exit fully before boarding. Aligning timing with collective rhythm rather than asserting individual priority. When uncertain, mirror nearby Japanese behaviour exactly. If they bow briefly when receiving change, repeat the gesture. If they remain silent in elevators, do likewise.

Social connection in Japan accumulates through reliable, low-stakes presence, not verbal declarations. Trust forms through predictable rhythms: the ramen regular who claims the same stool until the chef knows their order without asking, or the festival volunteer who carries the same mikoshi shrine annually, their consistent appearance noted through quiet recognition rather than explicit greeting.

Begin with foundational acts that signal respect. Bowing to the convenience store clerk. Sorting trash correctly at the station. After sustained, visible effort, a neighbor might leave seasonal vegetables at a door without explanation. Accepting them with a slight bow and minimal words is connection, Japanese style.

Rituals for Guests

A particular stillness settles over visitors passing through a shrine gate in Japan. It hums quietly in the shift beneath the feet, in the hush of gravel under sandals. The pace slows automatically.

Shrines and tea rooms are invitations to soften, to take part in rituals offered in the same way for generations. At a Shinto shrine, the customs are simple but significant. Stopping at the purification basin to wash hands, then mouth, is about arriving clean in spirit, pausing before approaching something sacred. A coin is offered. A bow, a couple of claps, and another bow. It is rhythmic, but more importantly, it is a way of acknowledging presence.

The tea ceremony moves at a different pace but carries the same quiet weight. It teaches the concept of ma — meaningful pause — by guiding the body through deliberate stillness. Everything happens with care: the way the bowl is turned, the way the tea is whisked. Receiving the cup with both hands, turning it slowly, and drinking. It is not performative, and it is certainly not about the matcha. It is about intention, creating a shared moment.

Traditional Japanese arts demand presence, not talent. In Mashiko, a potter offers clay to anyone willing to try; in Kyoto, a calligrapher provides brush and ink to workshop attendees without asking credentials. These are systems entered through physical repetition, where understanding comes through the body before it reaches the mind. Ikebana conveys asymmetry by having practitioners position branches until negative space feels instinctively correct.

The Ryokan Experience

Staying at a ryokan is stepping into a different rhythm of life. From slipping off shoes at the entrance to being shown to a room with soft-spoken grace, guests participate in a deeply rooted cultural experience designed around comfort, quiet, and mutual consideration.

The room is intentionally simple: tatami floors, sliding doors, a low table with green tea. There is room to breathe. The details are thoughtful: a yukata neatly folded, cushions placed precisely, a seasonal flower in a small alcove. Everything is arranged for ease without drawing attention to itself.

The onsen — the communal bath — is where nerves often surface for first-time visitors. Bathing naked around strangers can feel uncomfortable initially, but the realization comes quickly that no one is watching. The protocol protects the space and the shared serenity within it: rinse thoroughly before entering the bath, tie up long hair, bring only a small towel, and never dip it in the water.

Mealtimes follow a quiet choreography. Multi-course dinners are

148

served in rooms or communal halls, encouraging diners to savour each bite — the flavours, presentation, textures, and pacing.

Festival Immersions

Experiencing Japan's regional festivals requires logistical precision, not spontaneous wandering. Most matsuri operate on strict calendars. Kyoto's Gion Matsuri unfolds throughout July, but its main yamaboko processions occur on July seventeenth and twenty-fourth. Missing one means waiting a year.

Festivals invite hands-on participation. Koenji Awa Odori in late August is among the most accessible entry points. Beginner workshops run in the days before the main procession, where thousands learn the dance's distinctive posture — one arm raised, one low, knees bent, the body tilting forward into a gliding walk that looks effortless and feels anything but. By the time the procession moves through the covered shopping arcade under rows of paper lanterns, the distinction between seasoned dancer and first-timer has largely dissolved into collective rhythm. Regional matsuri actively recruit visitors to shoulder mikoshi portable shrines or help with setup — participation that addresses genuine community needs while offering cultural immersion. Kanamara Matsuri in Kawasaki explicitly welcomes foreigners into its unconventional celebration, creating space for outsiders within sacred ritual.

Local organisers distribute happi coats, demonstrate protocols through gesture rather than translation, and position newcomers beside experienced carriers who guide through physical correction. The procession moves through narrow streets where entire neighborhood emerge: grandmothers clapping rhythms, children distributing blessed rice, shopkeepers offering water stations. This is living tradition absorbing participants into its annual rhythm, where effort matters more than understanding.

Sincerity over Perfection

Physical boundaries matter in sacred spaces. An awkward bow during a tea ceremony or a towel accidentally dipped in the onsen bath requires quiet correction, not effusive apology. Adjusting posture, restoring silence, and continuing is the expected response. Japanese etiquette forgives sincere mistakes but recognizes performative ignorance.

When language fails during temple meditation, becoming a mirror is the most effective strategy. Matching the posture of the person beside you — their breathing rhythm, the precise timing of their bows, the angle of their spine. Zen practitioners understand that embodied presence speaks louder than words.

Serious missteps demand different responses. Photographing where forbidden, speaking loudly in sacred silence, or tracking shoes past the genkan threshold require a bowed head and immediate cessation. Skipping the verbal apology in English avoids creating conversational burden. The body admits fault, and subsequent behaviour demonstrates understanding.

Sitting through discomfort teaches what words cannot: endurance without complaint, learning through correction rather than retreat. To maintain its deepest traditions while welcoming millions of strangers every year, the culture relies on the quiet power of observation.

Epilogue: The Invitation

T HERE IS A MOMENT that happens to almost every traveler in Japan, usually somewhere in the middle of the trip, when the country stops being a place you are visiting and starts being a place you are inside. It doesn't announce itself. It arrives quietly, the way most important things in Japan do.

Maybe it happens at a train station, when you realize you have been navigating the platform signs without consciously reading them. Maybe it happens at a konbini at two in the morning, when the clerk bows and says irasshaimase and you bow back without thinking. Maybe it happens at a shrine, when you find yourself pausing at the torii gate — not because a guidebook told you to, but because something in you has learned that the pause matters.

That moment is not about fluency. It is not about expertise. It is about attention.

Japan is a country that rewards attention more than almost anywhere else on earth. The perfectly folded receipt. The train that arrives at 7:43 and not 7:44. The ramen shop owner who has been perfecting the same broth for thirty years and still believes he has not quite gotten it right. These are not quirks or tourist attractions. They are a philosophy made visible — the idea that the way you do a thing is inseparable from the thing itself.

This book has tried to give you the context to see that philosophy clearly. The history that shaped it. The social architecture that sustains it. The paradoxes that make it human rather than mechanical.

But context is only the beginning. The real work happens when you arrive.

You will make mistakes. You will bow at the wrong moment, or not bow when you should, or hold your chopsticks incorrectly, or walk on the wrong side of the footpath. None of this matters as much as you fear it will. The Japanese have been receiving foreign visitors for centuries and they understand, with characteristic patience, that the learning takes time. What they notice — what they quietly appreciate — is not perfection. It is effort. It is the willingness to try.

Respect the invisible labor. The perfectly aligned bento boxes at a train station kiosk didn't arrange themselves. The person who handed you your change with two hands and a bow doesn't see themselves as "just" a cashier. Small acts of acknowledgment — a nod, a quiet arigatou gozaimasu, a moment of hesitation before snapping a photograph — are your way of bowing back.

Don't rush. There is an impulse, especially for travelers trying to see it all, to cram too much into each day. Japan rewards those who linger — who sit quietly under a tree at a shrine instead of just snapping a picture, who watch the rhythm of a neighborhood konbini rather than sprinting to the next must-see. Locals notice when you are present, not just passing through.

The chapters you have read cover a great deal of ground. But Japan is not a country you finish. It is a country you return to, and each return reveals something the previous visit obscured. The traveler who comes back after ten years finds that the surface has shifted — new buildings, new fashions, new technology — while something underneath has remained entirely still. That stillness is what you are really traveling toward.

And maybe that's the real secret: Japan isn't asking you to be perfect. But it is offering you an invitation — to slow down, to notice, to meet precision with presence. The invitation is open-ended. It doesn't expire when your visa does. It travels home with you, in the way you start to notice the quality of silence in a room, or the care someone has taken with something small, or the particular satisfaction of a thing done exactly right.

If you can accept that invitation, you won't just visit Japan.

You'll connect with it.

Chapter Eighteen

Appendix A

Everyday Japanese Phrases

YOU DO NOT NEED a long vocabulary list to navigate Japan. You only need a handful of the right phrases, offered sincerely. Politeness in Japanese relies heavily on consideration and timing rather than perfect grammar. A slight bow and a well-timed greeting can accomplish as much as a fluent sentence. Even the simplest phrases carry weight when spoken kindly.

Here is a core set of essentials, useful everywhere from train stations to temple grounds.

The Foundation

Sumimasen (soo-mee-mah-sen) — Excuse me / I'm sorry / Thank you

This is the Swiss Army knife of Japanese phrases. You will hear it constantly and use it daily. Say it to get a waiter's attention, to apologize lightly if you bump into someone on the subway, or to express thanks when someone holds a door for you. Using it with a small bow or nod softens the interaction every time.

Arigatou gozaimasu (ah-ree-gah-toe go-zah-ee-mah-soo) — Thank you (polite)

Use this in nearly every formal interaction — when paying at a convenience store, receiving help at a hotel desk, or accepting a purchase. A warm arigatou opens doors.

Onegaishimasu (oh-neh-guy-shee-mah-soo) — Please / I would like this

This phrase politely requests an item or an action. Use it when ordering food, handing over your credit card, or asking a favor. If you point to an item on a menu and say onegaishimasu, the interaction is complete and polite.

Daijoubu desu (die-joe-boo des) — It's okay / I'm fine / No, thank you

Highly adaptable. Use it to decline a plastic bag at a store, to reassure someone if you drop something, or to respond if asked whether you need assistance.

Wakarimashita (wah-kah-ree-mah-shee-tah) — Understood / Got it

A useful phrase to confirm you have understood directions, instructions, or rules. It helps close an exchange smoothly.

Yoroshiku onegaishimasu

(yoh-roh-shee-koo oh-neh-guy-shee-mah-soo)

— Please treat me well / Thanks in advance

There is no clean English equivalent for this phrase, which is part of why it is worth knowing. It carries a blend of humility, gratitude, and goodwill. You will hear it at the end of introductions, at hotel check-ins, and whenever someone is asking another person to help them with something. Saying it at the right moment signals that you understand how Japanese social exchange works.

Chotto matte kudasai (cho-toe maht-teh koo-dah-sigh) — Please wait a moment

Helpful when you need a second to find your wallet, gather your thoughts, or locate your ticket at a gate.

Eigo o hanasemasu ka? (ay-go oh hah-nah-seh-mahs kah) — Do you speak English?

Not everyone does, but asking in Japanese before switching to English shows immediate respect. Combine this with a smile and slow gestures if needed.

Greetings and Acknowledgments

In Japan, greetings are everyday rituals. A well-placed morning greeting is a way of acknowledging the people around you and the rhythm of the day. These phrases act as small bridges, helping you connect even when you lack a shared language.

Ohayou gozaimasu (oh-hah-yoh go-zah-ee-mah-soo) — Good morning

Used until around 11:00 AM. Appropriate for hotel staff, people you pass on a hiking trail, or the owner of the guesthouse where you are staying.

Konnichiwa (kohn-nee-chee-wah) — Good afternoon / Hello

Simple, classic, and appropriate throughout the middle of the day.

Konbanwa (kohn-bahn-wah) — Good evening

Use this as the sun sets, perhaps when walking into a small restaurant or passing someone in a quiet neighborhood.

Oyasuminasai (oh-yah-soo-mee-nah-sigh) — Good night

Best used at the very end of the evening, when leaving a bar or saying goodnight to innkeepers.

Dining and Food

Osusume wa nan desu ka? (oh-soo-soo-meh wah nahn des kah) — What do you recommend?

A great way to invite a personal touch from restaurant staff, especially when a menu is overwhelming or written entirely in Japanese.

Okaikei onegaishimasu (oh-kye-kay oh-neh-guy-shee-mah-soo) — Check, please

Use this with a small nod or raised hand when you are ready to pay. In most Japanese restaurants, you take the bill to the register at the front rather than paying at the table.

Itadakimasu (ee-tah-dah-kee-mah-soo) — Said before eating

This translates roughly to "I humbly receive." Saying it before a meal is a deep-seated cultural habit, acknowledging the effort of the cook and the life of the ingredients. You will hear it at every table.

Gochisōsama deshita (go-chee-so-sah-mah desh-tah) — Said after eating

Say this to the chef as you leave a ramen counter or to the staff as you exit a restaurant. It is one of the most appreciated phrases a foreign visitor can use.

Kanpai! (kahn-pie) — Cheers!

The essential phrase for any izakaya visit. Wait for someone to say it before you drink — raising your glass and sipping before the kanpai is considered poor form. When in doubt, hold your glass slightly lower than the person you are toasting with, especially if they are older.

Travel and Directions

Eki wa doko desu ka? (eh-kee wah doh-koh des kah) — Where is the train station?

You can swap out eki (station) for almost anything: toire (toilet), hoteru (hotel), or konbini (convenience store).

Toire wa doko desu ka? (toy-reh wah doh-koh des kah) — Where is the toilet?

Worth having ready on its own. Japan's public restrooms are excellent, but they are not always obvious from the street.

Ikura desu ka? (ee-koo-rah des kah) — How much is this?

Essential in markets, craft shops, and anywhere without clear pricing. Point to the item and ask.

Kono densha wa Tokyo e ikimasu ka? (koh-no den-shah wah tokyo eh ee-kee-mahs kah) — Does this train go to Tokyo?

Extremely useful when navigating complex transfers. Point to the train and ask a station attendant or fellow passenger.

Kore kudasai (koh-reh koo-dah-sigh) — This one, please

Ideal in shops, bakeries, or food stalls. Point to what you want and say this phrase.

When You Need More Time

Mō ichido onegaishimasu (moh ee-chee-doh oh-neh-guy-shee-mah-soo) — One more time, please

When someone speaks too fast or you miss something. Polite, clear, and always understood.

Yukkuri hanashite kudasai (yoo-koo-ree hah-nah-shee-teh koo-dah-sigh) — Please speak slowly

Invaluable when trying to follow directions or understand a response. Most people will immediately adjust their pace, often with a smile.

Nani? / Nan desu ka? (nah-nee / nahn des kah) — What? / What is it?

Nani is casual and quick. Nan desu ka is the polite version. Use the latter when asking for clarification from a stranger or in any formal setting.

Smoothing the Edges

There is a certain rhythm to everyday Japanese that acts as the soft glue holding conversations together. Learning a few of these in-between sounds helps you navigate interactions more naturally.

Eeto... (eh-toh) — Um...

Used to buy time or signal you are thinking. Considered much more polite than dead silence.

Sou desu ne (soh des neh) — Hmm, yes... / I see what you mean

A gentle agreement or reflection. You will hear this constantly in shops and conversations as a way of showing active listening.

Chotto... (cho-toe) — A little...

Infinitely useful. It can mean "a bit," "kind of," or serve as a polite refusal. If someone offers you something you cannot accept, saying chotto... while trailing off and smiling apologetically is the standard way to say "no" without causing offense.

Having these phrases ready shows respect, preparedness, and curiosity. Locals appreciate the effort, and you will find that interactions become warmer and more connected when you use even a few of them sincerely. Because in Japan, how you say something often matters as much as what you say.

Chapter Nineteen

Appendix B

Books, Films & Cultural Resources

What to Read, Watch, and Listen To

JAPAN'S CULTURAL DEPTH DOESN'T end when your trip does — in fact, it often begins there. Whether you're curled up with a novel, watching a late-night film, or tuning into a podcast on your commute, exploring Japanese culture through media opens windows you might've missed on the ground. This list isn't exhaustive or academic — it's personal, practical, and designed to deepen your connection to Japan, no matter where you are.

Books (in English or translated from Japanese)

- *Norwegian Wood* by Haruki Murakami – A lyrical, melancholic novel that blends the personal with the universal. A gateway into modern Japanese literature.

- *Convenience Store Woman* by Sayaka Murata – A quietly subversive look at identity, work, and social expectation, all from inside a konbini.

- *The Book of Tea* by Kakuzō Okakura – Written in English in 1906, it's still one of the best reflections on aesthetics, ritual, and philosophy in Japan.

- *A Geek in Japan* by Héctor García – A smart, visual introduction to contemporary Japanese culture through an outsider's lens.

Films

- *Spirited Away* (Hayao Miyazaki) – A modern animated classic, deeply rooted in folklore, Shinto imagery, and childhood wonder.

- *Tokyo Story* (Yasujiro Ozu) – Quiet, contemplative, and deeply moving — a masterclass in stillness and generational tension.

- *Departures* (Yōjirō Takita) – A touching exploration of life, death, and dignity, centered on the art of the Japanese funeral ritual.

Music & Audio

- *Joe Hisaishi's Film Scores* – If you've seen a Studio Ghibli film, you've likely heard his music. Gentle, emotional, unforgettable.

- *City Pop* (artists like Tatsuro Yamashita or Mariya Takeuchi) –

Japan's nostalgic, upbeat sound from the 80s that's had a global comeback.

- *Koto and Shakuhachi music* – Traditional Japanese instruments that evoke the stillness of temples and tea rooms.

These are cultural touchstones — not just entertainment, but lenses. They don't explain Japan. They offer a feeling, a texture, a way in.

From Manga to Memoir – A Curated Guide

Not all stories are told the same way — and in Japan, some of the most revealing windows into culture come through frames of ink, autobiography, or quiet observation. Manga, graphic novels, and personal essays carry emotional weight and social commentary, often with far more nuance than they're credited for. Whether you're new to these formats or deep into the genres, here's a curated selection that blends entertainment with insight.

Manga with Cultural Depth

- *My Brother's Husband* by Gengoroh Tagame – A powerful, tender manga about family, acceptance, and cultural difference. LGBTQ themes meet traditional family dynamics with surprising warmth.

- *Barakamon* by Satsuki Yoshino – A charming series about a calligrapher who moves to a rural island, learning life lessons from quirky locals.

- *Showa: A History of Japan* by Shigeru Mizuki – A sweeping manga-style history, blending autobiography with national events. History class has never been this human.

Memoirs and Personal Stories

- Azuma Hiroki's *Otaku: Japan's Database Animals* – A philosophical dive into anime, consumerism, and postmodern identity in

Japan. Academic, but readable.

- *Tokyo Vice* by Jake Adelstein – A gripping memoir from a foreign crime reporter inside the world of Tokyo's underbelly. Part thriller, part cultural diary.

- *The Inland Sea* by Donald Richie – A poetic travel memoir written in the 1970s that captures the soul of lesser-seen Japan with wit and affection.

Graphic Storytelling That Travels

- *A Journal of My Father* by Jiro Taniguchi – A visual novel exploring grief, memory, and the generational gap in postwar Japan.

- *Yotsuba&!* by Kiyohiko Azuma – Lighthearted, childlike, and full of everyday charm. Through a little girl's eyes, the mundane becomes magical.

These works remind us that culture doesn't always arrive in lecture halls. Sometimes, it sneaks in through speech bubbles, diary pages, and watercolor panels — and stays with us long after.

Museums, Websites, and Cultural Deep Dives

Not everyone can stroll through the halls of a Kyoto museum or peer at a centuries-old scroll in person — but luckily, Japan's cultural treasures aren't confined to physical walls. Whether you're planning a future trip or simply curious from home, there are countless ways to explore Japan's artistic and intellectual life. Some places offer silence and stillness; others buzz with virtual exhibits or creative chaos. All of them invite you in.

Step Into the Past — Museums That Matter

Let's start with the big names: **The Tokyo National Museum** is where you go to meet Japan's past face-to-face. From delicate Heian-era calligraphy to armor that once belonged to real-life samurai, it's the kind of place that humbles you. If you can't visit in person, their online collection still offers that quiet thrill of discovery.

Over in Kyoto, the **Kyoto National Museum** speaks the language of elegance. You'll find exhibits that focus on the craftsmanship behind objects — things like lacquerware, Buddhist statuary, and ritual tools that were never meant to impress, only to endure.

Prefer something more playful? The **Ghibli Museum** in Mitaka is part storybook, part daydream. There's no straight-line tour — just winding rooms, hidden nooks, and glimpses into the minds that built Totoro's world. It's not a typical museum. It's an invitation to wonder.

Cultural Curiosity, Online and Ongoing

If your passport is digital for now, don't worry — Japan's cultural institutions have opened their archives to the world. The **Japan Foundation** has online galleries, films, and educational materials in English and Japanese. It's a fantastic place to wander through Japan's soft power: literature, film, and global dialogue.

Looking for something a bit more niche? The **Tsubouchi Theater Museum** (via Waseda University) is a goldmine for those fascinated by Japanese drama — Noh, Kabuki, and beyond. Their resources offer a sense of how performance has always been a reflection of social change.

For up-to-the-minute insights, **NHK World** and **Nippon.com** deliver high-quality journalism and mini-documentaries in English. They don't just explain Japan — they show it as it is, contradictions and all.

For the Deep Divers

Some sites reward curiosity with layers. **Tofugu** is a good example — part humor, part deep dive, it breaks down cultural quirks in a voice that's smart and weird in the best way. If you're more academically inclined, **JSTOR Japan Studies** offers peer-reviewed articles on everything from economic history to aesthetics. And **Kansai Digital**

Archives lets you time travel through Osaka, Nara, and Kyoto via digitized maps and photos.

Whether you're looking for a quiet museum hall, an animated interview, or a centuries-old ink drawing online, the tools to explore Japan are everywhere. The only thing you need is the willingness to look — and a bit of time to listen.

Living Language – Podcasts, YouTube, and Learning Resources

Language doesn't live in textbooks. It lives in cafes, on bullet trains, in overheard jokes, in the way someone says *"ehhh?"* with ten different meanings. To get a real feel for Japanese, you need to hear it breathing — with its rhythms, hesitations, and cultural pauses intact. Thankfully, the digital world offers more than enough chances to do just that, no plane ticket required.

Ears Open – Podcasts That Teach and Reveal

Start with "**JapanesePod101**" — not just a podcast, but a sprawling audio library. It has lessons for absolute beginners and casual learners, but also cultural tidbits that go beyond textbook phrases. It's practical, yes, but also full of real-life nuance: how to complain politely, how to refuse without offending, how to read between the lines.

For something more immersive, "**Let's Learn Japanese from Small Talk**" is hosted by two native speakers chatting casually about everything from dating to seasonal foods. They don't slow down. They don't over-explain. That's the point — it's how people actually speak. You might not catch every word at first, but your ears will thank you later.

Eyes Open – YouTube Channels Worth Following

On YouTube, "**Japanese Ammo with Misa**" breaks down grammar with a sense of humor and a ton of cultural context. Misa doesn't just tell you what a phrase means — she explains why it's said that way, and when you definitely shouldn't use it.

"**Tokini Andy**" offers longer grammar lessons using the Genki textbooks, perfect for learners who like structured progression. His tone is friendly and easygoing — like a class you actually want to show up for.

Then there's **Abroad in Japan**, a channel where British YouTuber Chris Broad shares cultural commentary, regional travel, and sarcastic takes on daily life. It's not a language-learning channel per se, but it's gold for cultural fluency and humor.

Learning by Living (Even from Afar)

Language study apps like **WaniKani** (for kanji) and **BunPro** (for grammar practice) are useful, especially if you're a goal-oriented learner. They help you track progress without getting overwhelmed.

But don't forget the quiet power of listening. Watch a drama. Follow a food vlogger. Read the subtitles — then try watching without them. Sit with the sounds. Mimic a line out loud. You don't need to speak perfectly. You just need to stay curious.

Because language, like culture, isn't something you conquer. It's something you enter — with care, humility, and joy.

Chapter Twenty

Appendix C

Travel and Etiquette Quick Tips

Packing for the Seasons, Traveling with Respect

P ACKING FOR JAPAN ISN'T just about the weather — it's about understanding that how you show up in public is a form of quiet communication. In a place where attention to detail runs deep, arriving prepared is a small but meaningful way to participate in the culture with respect.

The seasons, of course, shape everything. Spring can be soft and floral or surprisingly brisk, while autumn brings cool air and bursts of color. Both seasons call for layers — a light coat, something breathable underneath, and always a compact umbrella. You'll blend in best if you favor clean lines and muted tones over flashy colors or logos. Not because anyone will say anything if you don't — but because there's beauty in subtlety here, and people notice how you carry yourself.

Summer in Japan feels like walking through a warm bath. It's humid, relentless, and not for the faint of wardrobe. Bring breathable fabrics, a folding fan or cooling towel, and don't forget sun protection. A small hand towel in your bag isn't over-prepared — it's what locals do. You'll need it, trust me.

Winter, especially up north or in mountainous regions, means business. You'll want gloves, thermal layers, and shoes that can take on wet pavement or icy temple steps. Japan isn't extreme about outdoor fashion, but it does favor practicality — think less ski-resort glam, more quiet preparedness.

A quick tip: shoes matter. You'll take them off more than you expect — entering homes, temples, certain restaurants. Make sure they're easy to slip off and on, and always wear decent socks. You don't need to impress, but a little care speaks volumes.

And above all? Pack with space — in your suitcase and your mindset. Japan rewards travelers who leave a little room for the unexpected.

Do's and Don'ts from Shrines to Subways

Japan doesn't hand you a list of rules when you land. It hands you a rhythm — soft-spoken, precise, and deeply considerate. The best way to keep up? Watch. Listen. Let the place teach you how to move through it.

At a Shinto shrine, don't just breeze through the torii gate like it's decoration. Pause. It's not about ceremony — it's about presence. A small bow before entering signals that you know you're stepping into sacred space. Stay to the sides of the path; the center is for spirits, not selfies. You'll often find a water basin near the entrance. You're not expected to perform it like a ritual expert, but rinsing your hands — and sometimes your mouth — with the ladle is a quiet way to show respect.

Temples ask for a different kind of silence. No applause at the altar, no shouting across the courtyard. Incense smoke hangs thick and slow, and so should you. If you light a stick, fan the smoke toward you — toward your hands, your heart, whatever needs healing. Then step back. Let the place hold its stillness.

Now shift scenes: the subway. Noisy? Not in Tokyo. It's a kind of moving hush. Keep your phone on mute, conversations low. Don't eat on the train unless it's a long-distance one. Wait for passengers to exit before you board. Stand in line, even when no one's watching — because someone always is, and because that's how the system stays kind.

You're not being judged by perfection here. You're being noticed for effort. That's what matters most.

Cultural Clues for First-Time Visitors

If Japan seems mysterious at first, it's not because people are hiding things — it's because meaning often lives between the lines. For first-time visitors, reading those quiet signals can make all the difference between being a guest and being a welcome one.

Take shoes, for instance. The moment you step into a private home, a traditional inn, or even some restaurants, you'll see the genkan — a lowered entryway where you remove your shoes. It's not negotiable. If slippers are offered, take them. But if there's a sign to leave slippers at the bathroom door? Do. Some places even have special toilet slippers — and no, they don't leave the bathroom. Ever.

Elevators? Watch the dance unfold. The person nearest the buttons often takes the unspoken role of operator, pressing floor numbers for others and bowing slightly as people step in or out. It's not a job — it's a gesture.

When dining, resist the urge to pour your own drink. It's common to pour for others and let them return the favor. It's subtle, reciprocal, almost a language of care. Likewise, if you're clinking glasses, wait for someone to say kanpai! before you sip. And don't jab your chopsticks upright into a bowl of rice — that mirrors a funeral ritual and can come across as jarring.

But above all, be gentle. With your voice, your pace, your presence. Loud laughter, spreading out on public transport, or speaking over others will mark you more than any clothing or accent ever could.

Japan won't demand you get everything right. But it will quietly invite you to pay attention. That's how the conversation begins — not in words, but in the space between them.

Beyond the Guidebook – Things Locals Wish You Knew

It's easy to travel through Japan and feel like everything just works — the trains run on time, the streets are clean, the service is impeccable. But beneath that surface smoothness is a deep cultural engine powered by something less obvious: quiet effort. And many locals will tell you, the best travelers are the ones who notice that.

One thing many Japanese people appreciate is when visitors don't assume fluency — in English or otherwise. A small phrase in Japanese, even mispronounced, goes much further than speaking louder in your own language. A bow, a thank you, a moment of hesitation before snapping a photo — these things signal care. And care, in Japan, counts.

Don't rush. There's an impulse, especially for tourists trying to "see it all," to cram too much into each day. But Japan rewards those who linger — who sit quietly under a tree at a shrine instead of just snapping a picture, or who watch the rhythm of a neighborhood konbini rather than sprinting to the next must-see. Locals notice when you're present, not just passing through.

Respect the invisible labor. The perfectly aligned bento boxes at a train station kiosk didn't arrange themselves. The person who handed you your change with two hands and a bow doesn't see themselves as "just" a cashier. Small acts of respect — a nod, a quiet "arigatou gozaimasu" — are your way of bowing back.

S OME IDEAS CANNOT BE translated into a single English word without losing their shape. This is especially true in Japan, where culture and language are so deeply intertwined that certain concepts live more in atmosphere than in definition. This section offers a glimpse into a few of those terms — the ones that quietly govern behavior, design, and social interaction, even when they are never explicitly explained to visitors.

Learning them does more than build vocabulary. It builds an understanding of why things happen the way they do.

Cultural Coordinates

Wabi-Sabi (wah-bee sah-bee)

This is often reduced in the West to "rustic pottery" or "weathered wood," but that misses the point. Wabi-sabi is a way of seeing. It is the recognition of beauty in imperfection, grace in aging, and peace in simplicity. A chipped bowl repaired with gold (kintsugi), a silent room, a fallen leaf — wabi-sabi views these not as lacking or broken, but as complete in their impermanence. It is the aesthetic of the natural cycle.

Omotenashi (oh-moh-teh-nah-shee)

Usually translated as "hospitality," which feels far too transactional. Omotenashi is deeper and quieter. It is the kind of care that anticipates a need before it is voiced. A cup of tea served at the exact right temperature for the season, a door held open at the perfect moment, an umbrella offered before the rain starts. These gestures are made with no expectation of return or reward. They are done simply because it is the right way to treat a guest.

Gaman (gah-mahn)

The quiet endurance of hardship with dignity. It is the patience required to stand in a long queue without complaint, the resilience to rebuild after a disaster, and the emotional discipline to not burden others with your own frustration. Gaman is often what keeps the social fabric intact when systems are under stress.

Shikata ga nai (shee-kah-tah gah nigh)

Literally, "it cannot be helped." Westerners sometimes misread this as fatalism or apathy, but it is actually a mechanism for resilience. It is the conscious decision to accept what you cannot change — a delayed train, bad weather, a bureaucratic rule — so that you can move forward without wasting energy on anger. It is a kind of surrender that carries its own strength.

Kuuki wo yomu (koo-kee woh yoh-moo)

Literally, "reading the air." This is perhaps the single most important social skill in Japan. It means sensing the mood of a room, understanding what is left unsaid, and adjusting your behavior accordingly. If someone hesitates before answering a question, reading the air means understanding that their hesitation is actually a polite "no," and withdrawing the request before they are forced to say it aloud.

The Architecture of Conversation

Japanese is a "high-context" language. What is left unsaid often carries as much weight as the words actually spoken. To understand the cultural layer behind Japanese conversations, it helps to notice how language is used to protect harmony and show care without confrontation.

The Gentle No

Direct refusal is rare in polite Japanese society because it risks causing embarrassment or conflict. Instead, you will hear the word **chotto** (cho-toe — a little). If you ask for a favor and the response is, "That is chotto..." followed by a trailing silence and an apologetic smile, you have just been told no. In Japanese, this kind of indirectness is not considered evasive. It is considered empathetic.

The Art of Acknowledgment

Conversations in Japan are filled with sounds that might seem like filler to an outsider: ehh, **sou desu ne** (soh des neh — I see), **naruho-do** (nah-roo-hoh-doh — makes sense). These are called **aizuchi** (eye-zoo-chee). They are not interruptions; they are constant, rhythmic signals that the listener is paying attention. They give the speaker space and prove that they are being heard. Silence, in this context, would feel cold or disinterested.

The Weight of Names

Honorifics are the baseline of respect. Adding **-san** (sahn) after someone's name (e.g., Tanaka-san) is standard for adults in almost all social and professional settings. Using someone's name without an honorific — known as **yobisute** (yoh-bee-soo-teh) — is reserved exclusively for family members, partners, or very close friends. Doing it with a stranger or an acquaintance is jarringly disrespectful.

Formal, Casual, and Humble

One of the most complex aspects of Japanese communication is how the tone shifts depending on the relationship, the setting, and the hierarchy between the speakers.

At the heart of this is **keigo** (kay-go — honorific speech). Keigo actually has three distinct gears: **teineigo** (tay-neh-go — polite language for general use), **sonkeigo** (son-kay-go — respectful language used to elevate the person you are speaking to, like a customer or a boss), and **kenjougo** (ken-joe-go — humble language used to lower yourself in relation to them). You will hear deep keigo in department stores, at hotel front desks, and on train announcements. It is not just about being polite; it is about demonstrating social structure through grammar.

In casual settings, this architecture softens. Friends drop formal verb endings and speak in shorter, punchier rhythms. But casualness does not mean carelessness. Even informal Japanese has unspoken rules about not dominating the conversation or boasting.

Foreigners are almost always forgiven for missteps in this area. No one expects a visitor to master the nuances of keigo. But being aware of tone goes a long way. Understanding that the language shifts based on respect and relationship helps you see the invisible social currents flowing through every interaction. That is where real fluency begins — not with flawless grammar, but with the sensitivity to know when to bow, when to laugh, and when to simply pause.